AMERICAN PHOTOGRAPHY

T E N

CHAIRMAN: ROBERT PRIEST · DESIGNER: MATTHEW DRACE · PRODUCTION MANAGER: JONATHAN CHERNES · JACKET PHOTOGRAPH: RAYMOND MEEKS · PUBLISHER: KENNETH FADNER · DIRECTOR: MARK HEFLIN · JACKET COPY AND CHAIRMAN INTERVIEW: PEGGY ROALF, NEW YORK · SPECIAL THANKS TO THE SCHOOL OF VISUAL ARTS FOR PROVIDING THE SPACE AND EQUIPMENT FOR THE AMERICAN PHOTOGRAPHY 10 JUDGING. · CAPTIONS AND ARTWORK IN THIS BOOK HAVE BEEN SUPPLIED BY THE ENTRANTS. WHILE EVERY EFFORT HAS BEEN MADE TO ENSURE ACCURACY, AMERICAN PHOTOGRAPHY DOES NOT UNDER ANY CIRCUMSTANCES ACCEPT ANY RESPONSIBILITY FOR ERRORS OR OMISSIONS. · IF YOU ARE A PRACTICING PHOTOGRAPHER OR STUDENT AND WOULD LIKE TO SUBMIT WORK TO THE NEXT ANNUAL COMPETITION WRITE TO: AMERICAN PHOTOGRAPHY, 5 EAST 16TH STREET, 11TH FLOOR, NEW YORK, NY 10003 USA. TELEPHONE: 212-647-0874. · THE PHOTOGRAPHS IN THIS BOOK WERE ORIGINALLY PUBLISHED IN CONSUMER, TRADE AND TECHNICAL MAGAZINES, PERIODICALS, NEWSPAPERS AND THEIR SUPPLEMENTS. OTHERS WERE PHOTOGRAPHED FOR ADVERTISEMENTS, PROMOTIONAL DESIGN, ANNUAL REPORTS, BOOKS, CD COVERS, CATALOGS, DIRECT MAIL, SELF-PROMOTION, OR WERE PERSONAL WORKS. · DISTRIBUTED IN THE UNITED STATES AND CANADA: D.A.P./DISTRIBUTED ARTS PUBLISHERS , 636 BROADWAY, 12TH FLOOR, NEW YORK, NY 10012 · ISBN 1-886212-00-7 · DISTRIBUTED IN THE UNITED KINGDOM AND FRANCE: INTERNOS BOOKS, 12 PERCY STREET, LONDON W1P 9FB · ISBN 1-873968-49-3 · BOOK TRADE FOR THE REST OF THE WORLD: HEARST BOOKS INTERNATIONAL, 1350 AVENUE OF THE AMERICAS, NEW YORK NY 10019 · ADDITIONAL COPIES AVAILABLE THROUGH: AMERICAN PHOTOGRAPHY, 5 EAST 16TH STREET, NEW YORK, NY 10003 · PRINTER: DAI NIPPON, HONG KONG · COPYRIGHT C 1994 AMILUS INC. · ALL RIGHTS RESERVED. NO PART OF THIS PUBLICATION MAY BE REPRODUCED, STORED IN A RETRIEVAL SYSTEM, OR TRANSMITTED IN ANY FORM OR BY ANY MEANS, ELECTRONIC, MECHANICAL, PHOTOCOPYING, RECORDING OR OTHERWISE, WITHOUT PRIOR PERMISSION OF THE COPYRIGHT OWNERS.

THE JURY

FABIEN BARON

Fabien Baron, originally from Paris, arrived in New York in 1982, first working at Condé Nast. In 1987 he designed the prototype of New York Woman, and was the magazine's art director for its first year. While at New York Woman he was appointed Creative Director of Barneys New York, producing award winning print campaigns for several years.

Mr. Baron has designed and developed advertising campaigns and packaging for some of the best known names in fashion, including Michael Kors, Calvin Klein, Valentino, Pucci, Lanvin, Norma Kamali, and Issey Miyake.

He designed Madonna's SEX, and directed the music video, Madonna's Erotica. Currently, he is Creative Director of Harper's Bazaar, relaunched in September 1992 and consulting Art Director of Calvin Klein. He continues to serve as President of his advertising and design studio, Baron & Baron. Acclaimed as one of the world's most provocative and revolutionary designers Mr. Baron and Harper's Bazaar was awarded a gold medal by the American Society of Magazine Editors. Most recently he was recognized with a special award for Influence in Art Direction by the Council of Fashion Designers of America (CFDA) in 1994.

STEPHEN DOYLE

Stephen Doyle, Creative Director of Drenttel Doyle Partners in New York, is best known for their typographic high jinks. The firm has tested their eclectic ideas in the realms of magazine and book design, marketing, packaging, corporate identity and advertising, as well as exhibition graphics and products.

Drenttel Doyle Partners handles such diverse clients as The Museum of Modern Art, Champion International, Warner Bros. Records, Wamsutta, The World Financial Center, The Equitable, The Cooper-Hewitt Museum, Wildlife Conservation Society, The Edison Project, Princeton and others.

Previously, Mr. Doyle was Art Director of M &Co., and designed at Rolling Stone and Esquire. He credits his collection of over 100 design awards to "really, really small type." His teaching posts include the graduate program at Yale and The Cooper Union. Mr. Doyle lives with his wife and two children in Greenwich Village.

MATTHEW DRACE

Matthew Drace was most recently the Design Director of Travel & Leisure where he had redefined the photographic language of travel magazines. Prior to his arrival at T&L, Mr. Drace was the Art Director and creative force behind the launch of Men's Journal published by Rolling Stone's parent company, Wenner Media. During his tenure at Men's Journal, the magazine received a nomination for a National Magazine Award for Design.

Before coming to New York, Mr. Drace lived in San Francisco, where he was Art Director of San Francisco Focus, and was widely recognized for his award winning designs and photographic treatments. Prior to this he was initiated into the wonderful world of magazines at D Magazine, in Dallas, Texas, where he was the Art Director. His creative work has earned him Gold and Silver medals from the Society of Publication Design and other organizations during his past 15 years in the industry.

Currently, while establishing Matthew Drace Design, Mr. Drace is consulting on several magazine and book projects. He resides in Manhattan, where he is decorating his new brownstone.

MICHAEL GROSSMAN

Michael Grossman is a partner and Creative Director of Meigher Communications, a new multimedia consumer publishing partnership whose products range from magazines (including Garden Design and Saveur) to software. He has designed, edited, and consulted for some 20 titles-from dailies to annuals; coffee-table books to comics; scholarly journals to CD-ROMS-for clients and employers as varied as Entertainment Weekly, National Lampoon, Sports Illustrated, Warner Books, The Village Voice, and Playboy. Among the over 150 awards his work has received are four National Magazine Award nominations-the first (for design) at the age of 21. During his five years as Design Director of Entertainment Weekly the magazine was nominated for two National Magazine Awards for design, named AdAge's Magazine of the Year, and three times cited as one of Adweek's "10 Hottest Magazines."

LAURIE KRATOCHVIL

Laurie Kratochvil has been involved in the world of photography for over twenty years. She began her career at the Los Angeles Times in 1974 and worked for numerous national publications before joining Rolling Stone in 1982. During her twelve years there, the magazine won every major photography prize including the National Magazine Award.

In addition to working on Rolling Stone, she has edited a number of books, including the New York Times best-seller, Rolling Stone: The Photographs. Laurie has curated several photography exhibitions in the United States and Europe; she is a frequent panelist and lecturer and has judged numerous photography competitions.

Currently, she is working on a book and exhibition of Albert Watson's photographs and Images of Rock & Roll , a photo-illustrated history of five decades of popular music, to be published by Little, Brown in 1995.

Ms Kratochvil, who is actively involved with Photographers + Friends United Against Aids, is a native of Newport Beach, California. She resides in New York City.

THE MEMORABLE AND CULTURE-DEFINING PUBLICATIONS ARE, IN A SENSE, BEYOND EDITION OF *AMERICAN PHOTOGRAPHY* PROVES TAKING AND THE SEARCH FOR TRUTH ARE THE PERFECTLY GOOD ONES. IT IS THE PHOTO PICTURE UNFORGETTABLE. • AN EVENTFUL BY THE RETURN OF RICHARD AVEDON'S STAGE. OUR JURY PLACED HIM IN THE COM SUCCESSORS, ALL OF WHOM SEEM TO IMBUE IMAGINATION. • THE JURORS WERE ASKED TO EACH PHOTOGRAPH BASED ON FIRST IMPRES CHOICES HAVE CREATED THIS ROBUST BOOK

PHOTOGRAPHS THAT ENLIVEN OUR CATEGORIZATION. OUR TENTH ANNUAL ONCE AGAIN THAT VITALITY AND RISK- WHAT SET GREAT IMAGES APART FROM GRAPHER'S POINT OF VIEW THAT MAKES A YEAR IN PUBLISHING WAS HIGHLIGHTED DYNAMIC STYLE TO THE EDITORIAL PANY OF HIS PEERS AND WOULD-BE THEIR WORK WITH INTELLIGENCE AND ACT ON IMPULSE - TO GIVE A VERDICT ON SION. WITH NO FURTHER EDITING, THEIR OF EXTRAORDINARY VISUAL POWER.

ROBERT PRIEST, CHAIRMAN

1 JOHN DUGDALE   ART DIRECTOR: GAEL TOWEY · DESIGNER: ANNE JOHNSON · PHOTO EDITOR: GAEL TOWEY · EDITOR: SUSAN WYLAND · PUBLICATION: MARTHA STEWART LIVING · PUBLISHER: TIME INC. · WRITER: CELIA BARBOUR · FOR THE ARTICLE, *CORN*, SEPTEMBER 1993.

3

2 **MARGARET BOURKE-WHITE** ART DIRECTOR: RUDOLPH C. HOGLUND · PHOTO EDITOR: MICHELE STEPHENSON · PUBLICATION: TIME · PUBLISHER: TIME INC. · COVER PHOTOGRAPH FOR THE FEATURE, *CAN RUSSIA ESCAPE ITS PAST?* DECEMBER 7, 1992. **3 JOHN DUGDALE** PUBLICATION: MARTHA STEWART LIVING, *CORN* **4,5 TORKIL GUDNASON** ART DIRECTOR: MATTHEW DRACE · ASSOCIATE ART DIRECTOR: GIOVANNI RUSSO · ASSOCIATE PHOTO EDITOR: ALLYSON TORRISI · EDITOR: JOHN RASMUS · PUBLICATION: MEN'S JOURNAL · PUBLISHER: WENNER MEDIA, INC. · WRITER: JOHN MCLAUGHLIN · FOR THE ARTICLE, *STOUT WORK*, JULY-AUGUST 1993 (FOLLOWING SPREAD).

6 MICHAEL THOMPSON CREATIVE DIRECTOR: FABIEN BARON · ART DIRECTOR: JOEL BERG · PUBLICATION: HARPER'S BAZAAR · PUBLISHER: HEARST PUBLICATIONS · WRITER: TINA GAUDOIN ·
SERIES FOR THE ARTICLE, *LIVING COLOR*, AUGUST 1993.

8

10

11

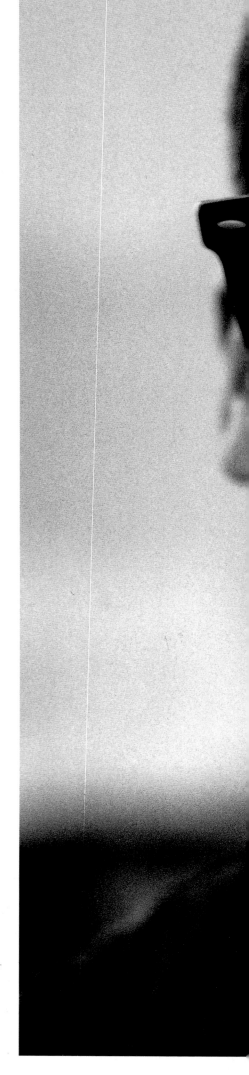

13 SEAN KERNAN *1994 BOOKS CALENDAR* **14 ANTON CORBIJN** PHOTO EDITOR: GREG POND · PUBLICATION: DETAILS · PUBLISHER: CONDÉ NAST PUBLICATIONS, INC. · WRITER: PAT BLASHILL · HENRY ROLLINS, FOR THE ARTICLE, *A FORCE OF ONE*, JANUARY 1994 **15 GUZMAN** PHOTO EDITOR: GREG POND · PUBLICATION: DETAILS · PUBLISHER: CONDÉ NAST PUBLICATIONS, INC. · WRITER: JOHN WEIR · FOR THE FEATURE, *THE BOYS AND THE BAN*, JUNE 1993(FOLLOWING SPREAD).

16-29 PEGGY SIROTA ART DIRECTOR: PAMELA BERRY • PHOTO EDITOR: JENNIFER CRANDALL • EDITOR: LAURA MORICE • PUBLICATION: US MAGAZINE • PUBLISHER: WENNER MEDIA, INC. • WRITER: STEVE POND • SERIES FOR THE FEATURE, *THIS OLDMAN, HE WEARS HATS*, OCTOBER 1993.

30 PEGGY SIROTA 31 MARK WEISS CREATIVE DIRECTOR: ROBERT PRIEST • PHOTO EDITOR: KAREN FRANK • PUBLICATION: GQ MAGAZINE • PUBLISHER: CONDÉ NAST PUBLICATIONS, INC. • WRITER: SCOTT OMELIANUK • SERIES FOR THE FEATURE *PATTERNS* ENTITLED, *ALL ABOUT SHIRTS*, DECEMBER 1993.

32-39 MARK WEISS **40 DAVID LACHAPELLE** PHOTO EDITOR: GREG POND • PUBLICATION: DETAILS MAGAZINE • PUBLISHER: CONDÉ NAST PUBLICATIONS • WRITER: ERIC HEDEGAARD • ACTRESS ROBIN JOI BROWN FOR THE ARTICLE, *BABES IN THE 'WOOD*, MARCH 1993 (FOLLOWING SPREAD).

41,42 TOM RYAN ART DIRECTOR: D.J. STOUT · PHOTO EDITOR: D.J. STOUT · EDITOR: GREGORY CURTIS · PUBLICATION: TEXAS MONTHLY · PUBLISHER: MEDIATEX COMMUNICATIONS · WRITER: ANNE DINGUS · SERIES FOR THE ARTICLE, *CREAM OF THE CROP,* MAY 1993.

43 LEN IRISH ART DIRECTOR: PAMELA BERRY • PHOTO EDITOR: JENNIFER CRANDALL • EDITOR: MAGGIE MURPHY • PUBLICATION: US MAGAZINE • PUBLISHER: WENNER MEDIA, INC. • WRITER: MARK COLEMAN • L.L. COOL J. FOR THE FEATURE, *COOL WORLD*, MARCH 1993. **44 ALASTAIR THAIN** ART DIRECTOR: MARK MICHAELSON • PHOTOGRAPHY DIRECTOR: MARY DUNN • PHOTO EDITOR: DORIS BRAUTIGAN • PUBLICATION: ENTERTAINMENT WEEKLY • PUBLISHER: TIME INC. • WRITER: JAMES KAPLAN • COVER AND INSIDE PHOTOGRAPH FOR FEATURE, *YOU DON'T KNOW JACK*, JANUARY 8, 1993. **45 LEN IRISH 46 ALASTAIR THAIN 47,48 MARY ELLEN MARK** ART DIRECTOR: PAMELA BERRY • PHOTO EDITOR: JENNIFER CRANDALL • EDITOR: SUSAN POCHARSKI • PUBLICATION: US MAGAZINE • PUBLISHER: WENNER MEDIA, INC. • WRITER: ROB TANNENBAUM • BOY GEORGE FOR THE FEATURE, *THE LOST BOY*, JUNE 1993.

49-55 DAN WINTERS ART DIRECTOR: D.J. STOUT • PHOTO EDITOR: D.J. STOUT • EDITOR: GREGORY CURTIS • PUBLICATION: TEXAS MONTHLY • PUBLISHER: MEDIATEX COMMUNICATIONS • WRITER: MIMI SWARTZ • (PRECEDING SERIES) FOR THE ARTICLE, *VIDOR IN BLACK AND WHITE*, DECEMBER 1993. **56 KEITH CARTER** ART DIRECTOR: JANE PALECEK • EDITOR: BRUCE KELLEY • PUBLICATION: HEALTH MAGAZINE • PUBLISHER: TIME INC. • WRITER: ANTHONY SCHMITZ • FOR THE ARTICLE, *SAY ALOHA TO HEALTH REFORM*, JULY-AUGUST 1993.

59

60

57-59 RODNEY SMITH · DESIGN DIRECTOR: MARCOS GAGO · SENIOR FASHION EDITOR: HEIDI GODOFF · PUBLICATION: MIRABELLA · PUBLISHER: MURDOCH MAGAZINES · FOR THE FASHION PORTFOLIO, *IDYLL IN NEUTRALS*, DECEMBER 1993. **60 RODNEY SMITH** CREATIVE DIRECTOR: DENNIS FREEDMAN · FASHION EDITOR: ROBERT BRYAN · PUBLICATION: W MEN'S PORTFOLIO · PUBLISHER: FAIRCHILDS PUBLICATIONS · FOR THE FASHION PORTFOLIO, *KEEP IT SIMPLE.*

61, 62 **MICHAEL WEINSTEIN** UNPUBLISHED SERIES FOR J. MORGAN PUETT.

63,64 **ALASTAIR THAIN** DESIGN DIRECTOR: GARY KOEPKE • ART DIRECTOR: RICHARD BAKER • PICTURE EDITOR: GEORGE PITTS • PUBLICATION: VIBE MAGAZINE • PUBLISHER: TIME INC. AND QUINCY JONES • WRITER: HILTON ALS • (PRECEDING SERIES) FOR *BETTER DAYS*, AN INTERVIEW WITH CHAKA KHAN. **65 RAYMOND MEEKS** ART DIRECTOR: MATTHEW DRACE • PUBLICATION: MEN'S JOURNAL • PUBLISHER: WENNER MEDIA, INC. • WRITER: RICK BASS • (FOLLOWING SERIES) ON ROMANIA FOR THE ARTICLE, *CREATURES OF THE DICTATOR*, APRIL 1994.

70-73 **KATHRIN MILLER** ART DIRECTOR: DAVID CARSON • PHOTO EDITOR: DAVID CARSON • EDITOR: MARVIN SCOTT JARRETT • PUBLICATION: RAY GUN • PUBLISHER: RAY GUN PUBLISHING,

INC. • SERIES FOR THE PORTFOLIO, *I HOPE I DIE BEFORE I GET OLD/RAY GUN VISITS LEISURE WORLD*, MARCH 1993.

74-76 JEAN LOUIS GREGOIRE PHOTO EDITOR: GREG POND • PUBLICATION: DETAILS • PUBLISHER: CONDÉ NAST PUBLICATIONS, INC. • FOR A FASHION DISPLAY, OCTOBER 1993.

79

77 EDWARD GAJDEL ART DIRECTOR: LOU DILORENZO · DIRECTOR OF PHOTOGRAPHY: BILL BLACK · PHOTO EDITOR: STEPHANIE SYROP AND KIRSTEN ROHRS · EDITOR: MARGARET STAATS SIMMONS · PUBLICATION: TRAVEL HOLIDAY · PUBLISHER: READER'S DIGEST PUBLICATIONS, INC. · WRITER: EDWARD GAJDEL · POET IRVING LAYTON OVER MONTREAL FOR THE FEATURE, *THE FRENCH CONNECTION*, JANUARY 1993(PRECEDING SPREAD). **78 HUGH HALES-TOOKE** PHOTOGRAPHY DIRECTOR: MARY DUNN · ASSISTANT PICTURE EDITOR: RAMIRO FERNANDEZ · PUBLICATION: ENTERTAINMENT WEEKLY · PUBLISHER: TIME INC. · WRITER: JESS CAGLE · LYPSINKA FOR THE ARTICLE, *MEMENTOS DEAREST-CHRISTIES AUCTIONS JOAN CRAWFORD'S TREASURES*, · JUNE 11, 1993. **79 MATTHEW ROLSTON** ART DIRECTOR: FRED WOODWARD · DESIGNERS: FRED WOODWARD, GAIL ANDERSON, DEBRA BISHOP, CATHERINE GILMORE-BARNES, GERALDINE HESSLER AND ANGELA SKOURAS · PHOTO EDITOR: LAURIE KRATOCHVIL · EDITOR: ROBERT B. WALLACE · PUBLICATION: ROLLING STONE TWENTY FIFTH ANNIVERSARY SPECIAL, *PORTRAITS*, NOVEMBER 12, 1992. · PUBLISHER: WENNER MEDIA, INC. · WRITER: GERRI HERSHEY · *SLASH*

80 GREGORY HEISLER CREATIVE DIRECTOR: ROBERT PRIEST • PHOTO EDITOR: KAREN FRANK • EDITOR: DAVID GRANGER • PUBLICATION: GQ MAGAZINE • PUBLISHER: CONDÉ NAST PUBLICATIONS, INC. • WRITER: SCOTT RAAB • TROY AIKMAN FOR THE ARTICLE, *THE SECOND COMING*, SEPTEMBER 1993. **81 JOHN REED FORSMAN** ART DIRECTOR: NANCY DUCKWORTH • PUBLICATION: LOS ANGELES TIMES MAGAZINE • PUBLISHER: TIMES MIRROR • *TOO MANY TOMATOES*, AUGUST 1993.

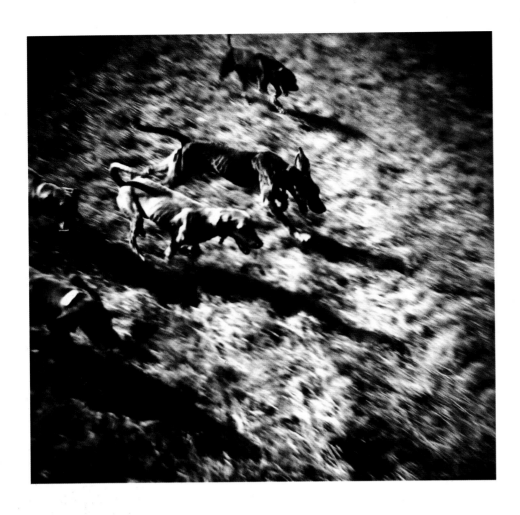

82 SCOGIN MAYO ART DIRECTOR: D.J. STOUT · PHOTO EDITOR: D.J. STOUT · EDITOR: GREGORY CURTIS · PUBLICATION: TEXAS MONTHLY · PUBLISHER: MEDIATEX COMMUNICATIONS · WRITER: ROBERT DRAPER · FOR THE ARTICLE, *MANHUNT AT MENARD CREEK*, OCTOBER 1993. **83 CHRISTINA GARCIA RODÉRO** ART DIRECTOR: NANCY DUCKWORTH · PHOTO EDITOR: LISA THACKABERRY · EDITOR: BRET ISRAEL · PUBLICATION: THE LOS ANGELES TIMES MAGAZINE · PUBLISHER: TIMES MIRROR · SERIES ENTITLED, *THE RITES OF SPRING*, APRIL 11, 1993.

84

84 JEFF MERMELSTEIN ART DIRECTOR: CHARLES CHURCHWARD • PHOTO EDITOR: SUSAN WHITE • EDITORS: MATTHEW TYRNAUER AND AIMEE BELL • PUBLICATION: VANITY FAIR •
PUBLISHER: CONDÉ NAST PUBLICATIONS, INC. • WRITER: DEBORAH MITCHELL • KALINKA AND LAUREN EZERSKY FOR *VANITIES, NEW YORK DIARY,* APRIL 1993. **85 ANDREW BRUSSO**
DESIGN DIRECTOR: MICHAEL GROSSMAN • PHOTOGRAPHY DIRECTOR: MARY DUNN • ASSISTANT PICTURE EDITOR: JULIE MIHALY • PUBLICATION: ENTERTAINMENT WEEKLY •
PUBLISHER: TIME INC. • WRITER: BRUCE FRETTS • FOR THE FEATURE, *WHO'S AFRAID OF HOWARD STERN?,* OCTOBER 15, 1993.

86 FRANK W. OCKENFELS 3 PHOTO EDITOR: DEBORAH NEEDLEMAN • PUBLICATION: THE WASHINGTON POST MAGAZINE • PUBLISHER: THE WASHINGTON POST COMPANY • *INAUGURATION*, JANUARY 1994 **87 FRANK W. OCKENFELS 3** PHOTO EDITOR: MARYANNE GOLON • PUBLICATION: TIME • PUBLISHER: TIME INC. • WRITER: PICO IYER • PORTRAIT OF PETER MATTHIESSEN FOR THE ARTICLE, *LAUREATE OF THE WILD*, JANUARY 11, 1993.

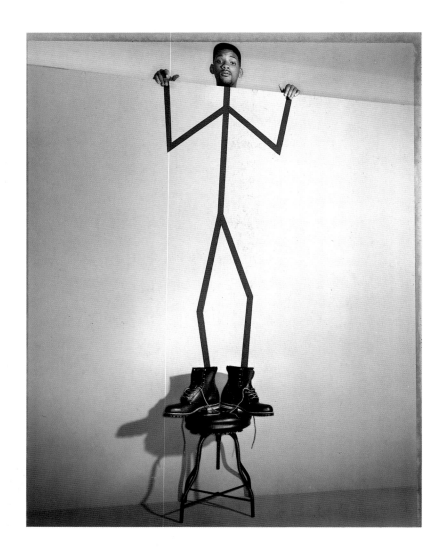

88 **DAN WINTERS** DESIGN DIRECTOR: MICHAEL GROSSMAN • PHOTOGRAPHY DIRECTOR: MARY DUNN • ASSISTANT PHOTO EDITOR: MARK JACOBSON • PUBLICATION: ENTERTAINMENT WEEKLY • PUBLISHER: TIME INC. • WILL SMITH, FOR THE ARTICLE, *COOL TRIPLE THREAT*, JUNE 25, 1993. 89 **SILVIA OTTE** ART DIRECTOR: B.W. HONEYCUTT • PHOTO EDITOR: GREG POND • PUBLICATION: DETAILS • PUBLISHERS: CONDÉ NAST PUBLICATION, INC. • COMMISSIONED, YET NOT PUBLISHED PORTRAIT OF GEORGE CLINTON.

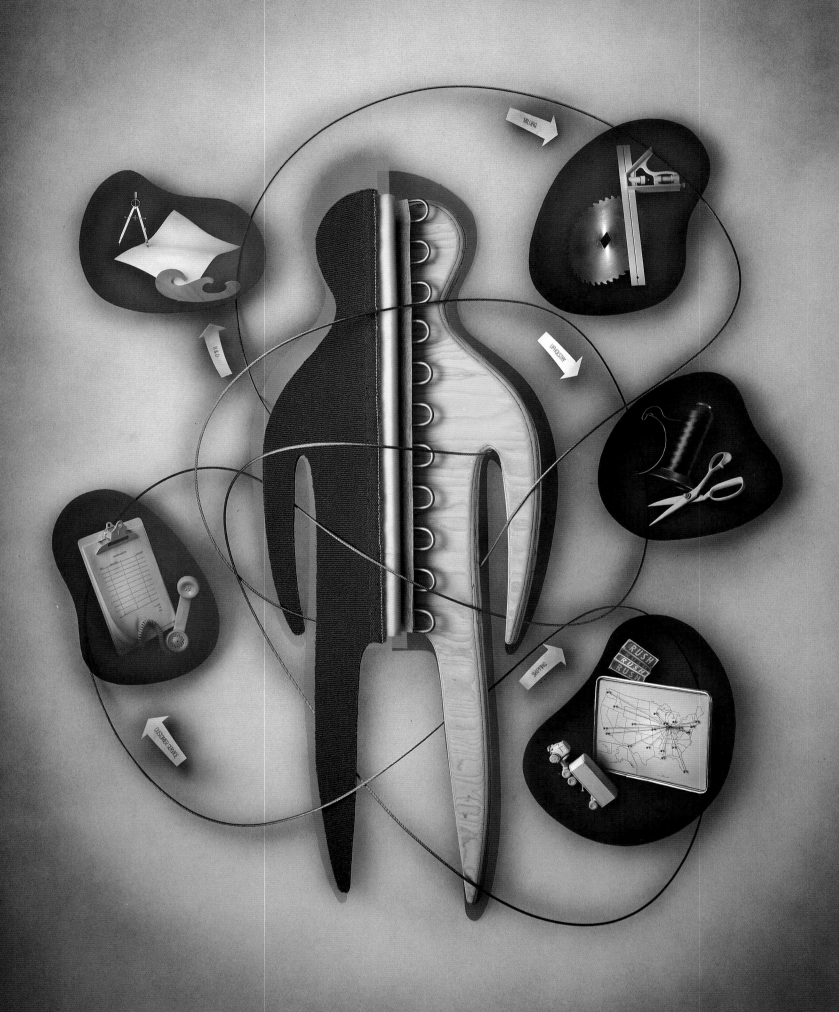

93

90 **HUGH KRETSCHMER** DESIGNER: NIEL POWELL · DESIGN FIRM: JOE DUFFY DESIGN · CLIENT: WIELAND FURNITURE COMPANY · AN INTERPRETATION OF THE COMPANY'S PHILOSOPHY: "COMMITMENT." 91,92 **RAYMOND MEIER** CREATIVE DIRECTOR: FABIEN BARON · ART DIRECTOR: JOEL BERG · PUBLICATION: HARPER'S BAZAAR · PUBLISHER: HEARST PUBLICATIONS · *PUNK ROCKS*, NOVEMBER 1993. 93,94 **PETER LINDBERGH** CREATIVE DIRECTOR: FABIEN BARON · ART DIRECTOR: JOEL BERG · PUBLICATION: HARPER'S BAZAAR · PUBLISHER: HEARST PUBLICATIONS · KRISTIE TURLINGTON FOR THE FEATURE, *LITTLE ME*.

95 RAYMOND MEIER CREATIVE DIRECTOR: FABIEN BARON • ART DIRECTOR: JOEL BERG • PUBLICATION: HARPER'S BAZAAR • PUBLISHER: HEARST PUBLICATIONS • WRITER: JON BOWERMASTER • SERIES FOR THE ARTICLE, *DIRE STRAITS*, JULY 1993. **96 MARIO SORRENTI** CREATIVE DIRECTOR: FABIEN BARON • ART DIRECTOR: JOEL BERG • PUBLICATION: HARPER'S BAZAAR • PUBLISHER: HEARST PUBLICATIONS • WRITER: TINA GAUDOIN • KATE MOSS FOR THE ARTICLE, *BODY OF EVIDENCE*, JULY 1993

97 RAYMOND MEIER CREATIVE DIRECTOR: FABIEN BARON • ART DIRECTOR: JOEL BERG • PUBLICATION: HARPER'S BAZAAR • PUBLISHER: HEARST PUBLICATIONS • WRITER: MIMI SHERATON • FOR THE ARTICLE, *SPOONING*, AUGUST 1993. **98,99 PAOLO ROVERSI** CREATIVE DIRECTOR: FABIEN BARON • ART DIRECTOR: JOEL BERG • PUBLICATION: HARPER'S BAZAAR • PUBLISHER: HEARST PUBLICATIONS • WRITER: SARAH MOWER • SERIES FOR THE FEATURE, *ARMANI AFTER DARK*, FEBRUARY 1993. **100 RAYMOND MEIER** PUBLICATION: HARPER'S BAZAAR, *DIRE STRAITS*

101 HORST STASNY ART DIRECTOR: MATTHEW DRACE • PHOTO EDITOR: ALLYSON TORRISI • EDITOR: JOHN RASMUS • PUBLICATION: MEN'S JOURNAL • PUBLISHER: WENNER MEDIA, INC. • WRITER: LAURENCE GONZALES • MONTANA'S GLACIER NATIONAL PARK, FOR THE ARTICLE *WILDEST AMERICA*, SEPTEMBER 1993. **102,103 SEBASTIAO SALGADO** ART DIRECTOR: FRED WOODWARD • PHOTO EDITOR: LAURIE KRATOCHVIL • PUBLICATION: ROLLING STONE • PUBLISHER: WENNER MEDIA, INC.

104-112 MARK SELIGER ART DIRECTOR: FRED WOODWARD · DESIGNERS: FRED WOODWARD, GAIL ANDERSON, DEBRA BISHOP, CATHERINE GILMORE-BARNES, GERALDINE HESSLER AND ANGELA SKOURAS · PHOTO EDITOR: LAURIE KRATOCHVIL · EDITOR: ROBERT B. WALLACE · PUBLICATION: ROLLING STONE TWENTY FIFTH ANNIVERSARY SPECIAL, *PORTRAITS*, NOVEMBER 12, 1992. · PUBLISHER: WENNER MEDIA, INC. · WRITER: GERRI HERSHEY. · *MICK FLEETWOOD & JOHN MCVIE, JOHNNY CASH, JEFF BECK, TOM PETTY, RINGO STARR, CARLOS SANTANA, DICKEY BETTS AND GREGG ALLMAN, BILLY JOEL, RAY DAVIES*

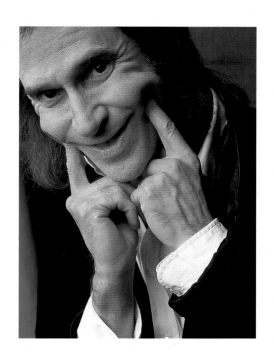

114

115,116 **HERB RITTS** LITTLE RICHARD, ARETHA FRANKLIN

117-120 DAVID ALLAN BRANDT CREATIVE DIRECTOR: KINSON CHAN · AGENCY: LIVE COMMUNICATIONS, LTD. · CLIENT: JEFFERY-WEST · COPYLINE: SEARCH FOR HIGHER GROUND.

121 DAVID LACHAPELLE PHOTO EDITOR: GREG POND · PUBLICATION: DETAILS MAGAZINE · PUBLISHER: CONDÉ NAST PUBLICATIONS, INC. · WRITER: ANKA RADAKOVICH · FOR AN INTERVIEW WITH TOM JONES, JULY 1993.

122 ALBERT WATSON PUBLICATION: ROLLING STONE TWENTY FIFTH ANNIVERSARY, PORTRAITS, *STEVE TYLER* **123-128 DANIEL BORRIS** ART DIRECTOR: KEVIN FISHER • PHOTO EDITOR: CYNTHIA VAN RODEN • EDITOR: RICK KAHL • PUBLICATION: SKIING MAGAZINE • PUBLISHER: TIMES MIRROR • WRITER: JOSH LERMAN • (FOLLOWING SERIES) FOR THE ARTICLE, *HUNTER'S HARD CORE*, JANUARY 1994.

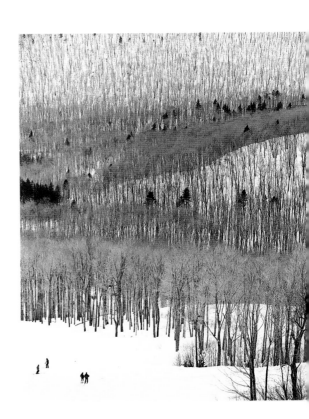

129 RAYMOND MEIER CREATIVE DIRECTOR: FABIEN BARON · ART DIRECTOR: JOEL BERG · PUBLICATION: HARPER'S BAZAAR · PUBLISHER: HEARST PUBLICATIONS · SERIES ENTITLED, *MYSTICAL JEWELS*, JUNE 1993. **130-132 DAVID ALLAN BRANDT** CREATIVE DIRECTOR: KINSON CHAN · AGENCY: LIVE COMMUNICATION, LTD. · CLIENT: BOY LONDON

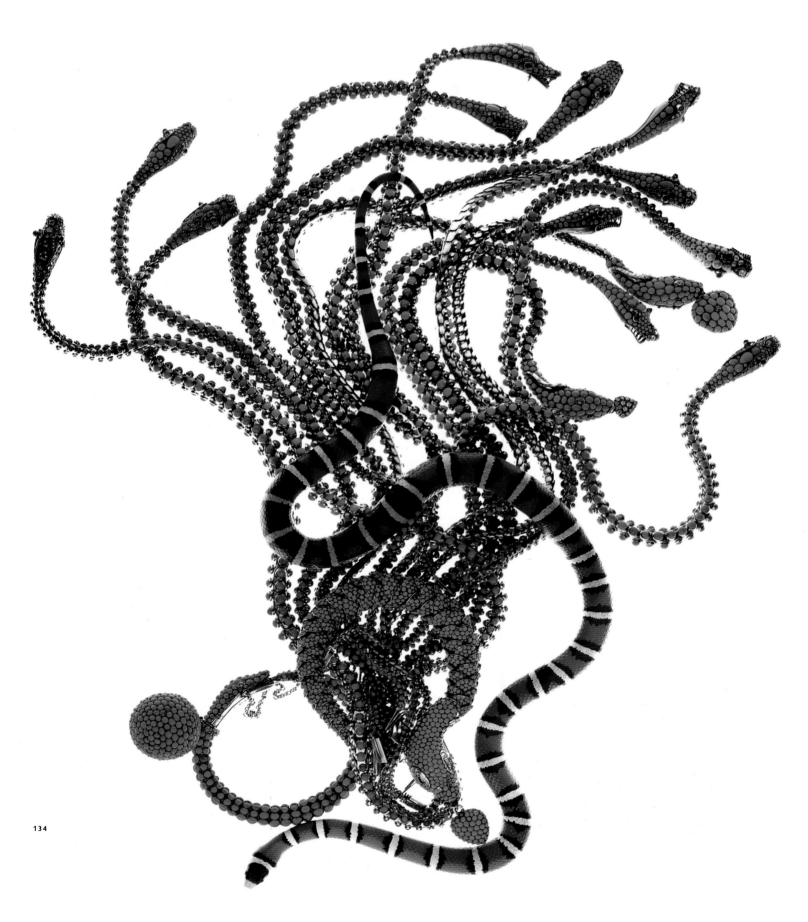

134

133 DANIEL PROCTOR DESIGNERS: AMY KNAPP AND MARY BRUCKEN • DESIGN FIRM: SBG PARTNERS • AUTHOR: FRANCO GALLI • PUBLISHER: CHRONICLE BOOKS • BOOK TITLE: THE IL FORNAIO BAKING BOOK, OCTOBER 1993. **134 RAYMOND MEIER** PUBLICATION: HARPER'S BAZAAR, *MYSTIC JEWELS*. **135 DANIEL PROCTOR** **136 KURT MARKUS** PUBLICATION: ROLLING STONE TWENTY FIFTH ANNIVERSARY, PORTRAITS, *JOHN LEE HOOKER*

137 DAVID LACHAPELLE PHOTO EDITOR: GREG POND · PUBLICATION: DETAILS · PUBLISHER: CONDÉ NAST PUBLICATIONS, INC. · *FAMILY MATTERS*, A SERIES OF "UP-AND -COMERS" AND THE PEOPLE WHO MADE THEM, JANUARY 1994. **138 DAVID LACHAPELLE** PHOTO EDITOR: GREG POND · PUBLICATION: DETAILS · PUBLISHER: CONDÉ NAST PUBLICATIONS, INC. · WRITER: SYLVIA PATTERSON · INTERVIEW WITH LEMONHEAD'S EVAN DANDO, JULY 1993. **139 DAVID LACHAPELLE** PHOTO EDITOR: GREG POND · PUBLICATION: DETAILS · PUBLISHER: CONDÉ NAST PUBLICATIONS, INC. · WRITER: ROGER TRILLING · PORN STAR MADISON, JUNE 1993. **140 BRUCE WEBER** PUBLICATION: ROLLING STONE TWENTY FIFTH ANNIVERSARY, PORTRAITS, *RICKIE LEE JONES*

141 BRUCE WEBER PUBLICATION: ROLLING STONE TWENTY FIFTH ANNIVERSARY, PORTRAITS, *RAY CHARLES* **142 CINDY SHERMAN** CREATIVE DIRECTOR: FABIEN BARON • ART DIRECTOR: JOEL BERG • PUBLICATION: HARPERS BAZAAR • PUBLISHER: HEARST PUBLICATIONS • WRITER: JIM LEWIS • SERIES FOR THE FEATURE, *THE NEW CINDY SHERMAN COLLECTION*, MAY 1993. **143,144 BRUCE WEBER** PUBLICATION: ROLLING STONE TWENTY FIFTH ANNIVERSARY, PORTRAITS, *ROBBIE ROBERTSON (FOLLOWING SPREAD)*.

147

145 **CINDY SHERMAN** PUBLICATION: HARPERS BAZAAR THE NEW CINDY SHERMAN COLLECTION **146,147 BRUCE WEBER** *MARIANNE FAITHFULL, SINEAD O'CONNOR*
148 **ALBERT WATSON** PUBLICATION: ROLLING STONE TWENTY FIFTH ANNIVERSARY, PORTRAITS, *JOHN LYDON*

149,150 KURT MARKUS ART DIRECTOR: JANET FROELICH • STYLIST: POLLY HAMILTON • PUBLICATION: THE NEW YORK TIMES MAGAZINE • PUBLISHER: THE NEW YORK TIMES
COMPANY • SERIES ENTITLED *A TIME FOR REVEALING*, MAY 16, 1993.

151

151-153 **KURT MARKUS** PUBLICATION: THE NEW YORK TIMES MAGAZINE, *A TIME FOR REVEALING*. 154 **MARK SELIGER** ART DIRECTOR: FRED WOODWARD ·
DESIGNERS: FRED WOODWARD AND GAIL ANDERSON · PHOTO EDITOR: LAURIE KRATOCHVIL · EDITOR: COREY SEYMOUR · PUBLICATION: ROLLING STONE · PUBLISHER:
WENNER MEDIA, INC. · WRITER: BRUCE PORTER · COCAINE SMUGGLER GEORGE JUNG FOR THE BOOK EXCERPT, *BLOW*, JULY 8, 1993. 155-158 **DAVID LACHAPELLE**
PUBLICATION: DETAILS, *FAMILY MATTERS*

163

162 DAN WINTERS ART DIRECTOR: JANET FROELICH • PHOTO EDITOR: KATHY RYAN • PUBLICATION: THE NEW YORK TIMES MAGAZINE • PUBLISHER: THE NEW YORK TIMES COMPANY • WRITER: LENA WILLIAMS • DENZEL WASHINGTON ON *MALCOLM X* FOR THE ARTICLE, *PLAYING WITH FIRE*, OCTOBER 25, 1992. **163 DAN WINTERS** ART DIRECTOR: FRED WOODWARD • PHOTO EDITOR: LAURIE KRATOCHVIL • PUBLICATION: ROLLING STONE • PUBLISHER: WENNER MEDIA, INC. • "CHRISTINE." UNPUBLISHED IMAGE FOR A SERIES ON WOMEN WHO STALK THE NIGHT STALKER. **164 NITIN VADUKUL** PHOTO EDITOR: GREG POND • PUBLICATION: DETAILS MAGAZINE • PUBLISHER: CONDÉ NAST PUBLICATIONS, INC. • WRITER: ROB TANNENBAUM • INTERVIEW WITH CHARLES BARKLEY, MAY 1993 (FOLLOWING SPREAD).

165 BRIAN SMALE ART DIRECTOR: FRED WOODWARD · DESIGNER: ANGELA SKOURAS · PHOTO EDITOR: LAURIE KRATOCHVIL · EDITOR: ERIC ETHERIDGE · PUBLICATION: ROLLING STONE · PUBLISHER: WENNER MEDIA, INC. · WRITER: JENNIFER ALLEN · FOR THE ARTICLE, *BOYS; HANGING WITH THE SPUR POSSE,* JULY 8, 1993.

167

166 MARK SELIGER ART DIRECTOR: PAMELA BERRY • PHOTO EDITOR: JENNIFER CRANDALL • EDITOR: LAURA MORICE • PUBLICATION: US MAGAZINE • PUBLISHER: WENNER MEDIA, INC. • WRITER: JEFF GILES • MICHAEL J. FOX, JULY 1993. **167 DAN WINTERS** PUBLICATION: TEXAS MONTHLY, *VICTOR IN BLACK AND WHITE*

171

168,169 WILLIAM MERCER MCLEOD *THE SCREAM · THE CHASE.* **170 DAN WINTERS** ART DIRECTOR: FRED WOODWARD · PHOTO EDITOR: LAURIE KRATOCHVIL · PUBLICATION: ROLLING STONE · PUBLISHER: WENNER MEDIA, INC. · COMMISSIONED, YET NOT PUBLISHED IMAGE OF DIRECTOR QUENTIN TARANTINO. **171 KIRSTIE LAIRD** *3 FOR FERGUSON*
171a TRIA GIOVAN FROM A FOUR YEAR PROJECT IN CUBA (FOLLOWING SPREAD).

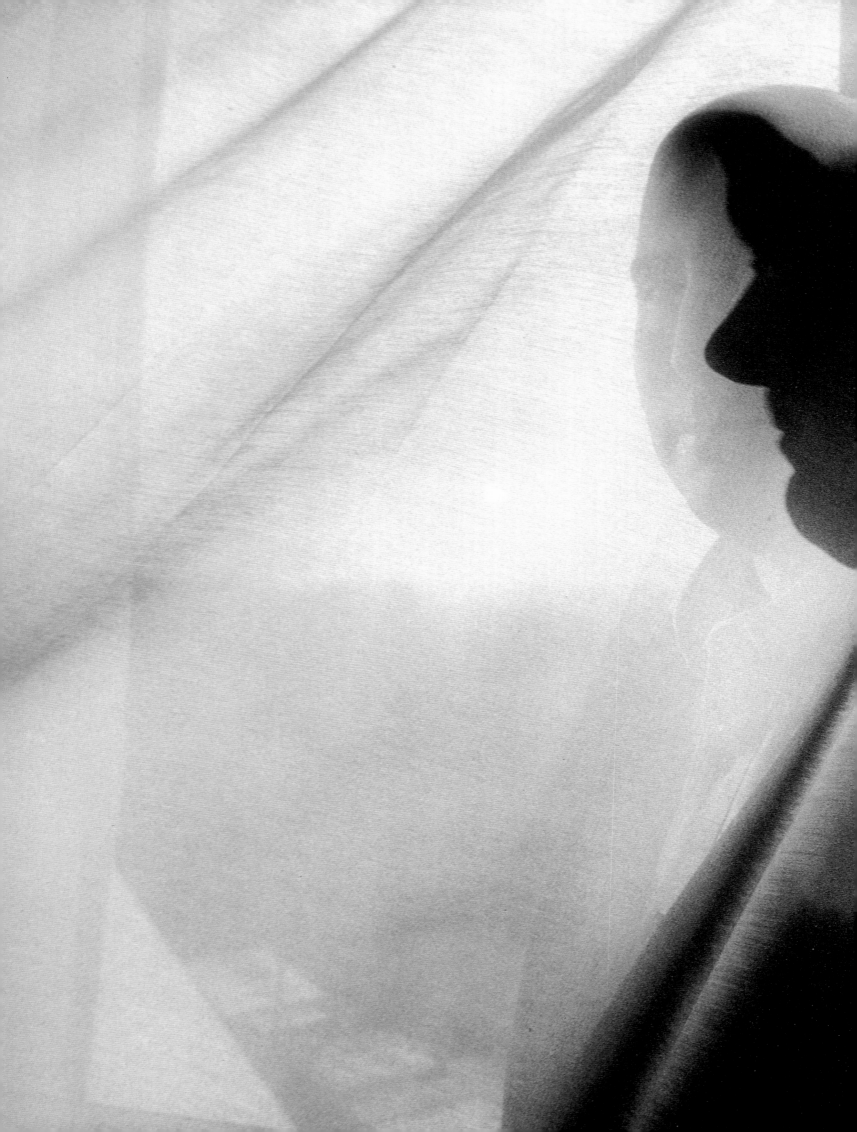

173

172 WILLIAM MERCER MCLEOD ART DIRECTOR: MICHAEL PICON · PHOTOGRAPHY DIRECTOR: MARY DUNN · PUBLICATION: ENTERTAINMENT WEEKLY · PUBLISHER: TIME INC.
· MYSTERY WRITER, PETER STRAUB (PRECEDING SPREAD). **173 CHRISTINA GARCIA RODÉRO** PUBLICATION: THE LOS ANGLES TIMES MAGAZINE, *THE RITES OF SPRING*

174-179 CHARLES MASON PHOTO EDITOR: PETER HOWE AND HOWARD CHAPNICK • EDITOR: HOWARD CHAPNICK • PUBLICATION: OUTTAKES, ISSUE #4 • WRITER: CHARLES MASON • SERIES FOR THE ARTICLE, *BLOOD AND VELVET*.

180-182 **KENNETH WILLARDT** ART DIRECTOR: DIANE AZIZA OOKA · PUBLICATION: PARENTING MAGAZINE · PUBLISHER: TIME INC. · SERIES ENTITLED *SOLES ON ICE*.
OCTOBER 1992

183

183 MIKE SALISBURY ART DIRECTOR: MIKE SALISBURY · EDITOR: GAIL HARRINGTON · PUBLICATION: AVENUE MAGAZINE · WRITER: LARRY DIETZ · ANTIQUE CAR SHOW FOR THE ARTICLE, *KAR KRAZY*, JANUARY 1994. **184 MICHEAL MCLAUGHLIN** CREATIVE DIRECTOR: ROBERT PRIEST · PHOTO EDITOR: KAREN FRANK · PUBLICATION: GQ MAGAZINE · PUBLISHER: CONDÉ NAST PUBLICATIONS, INC. · ADVOCATE EDITOR: JEFF YARBOROUGH FOR THE ARTICLE, *THE GAY PRESS*, MARCH 1993.

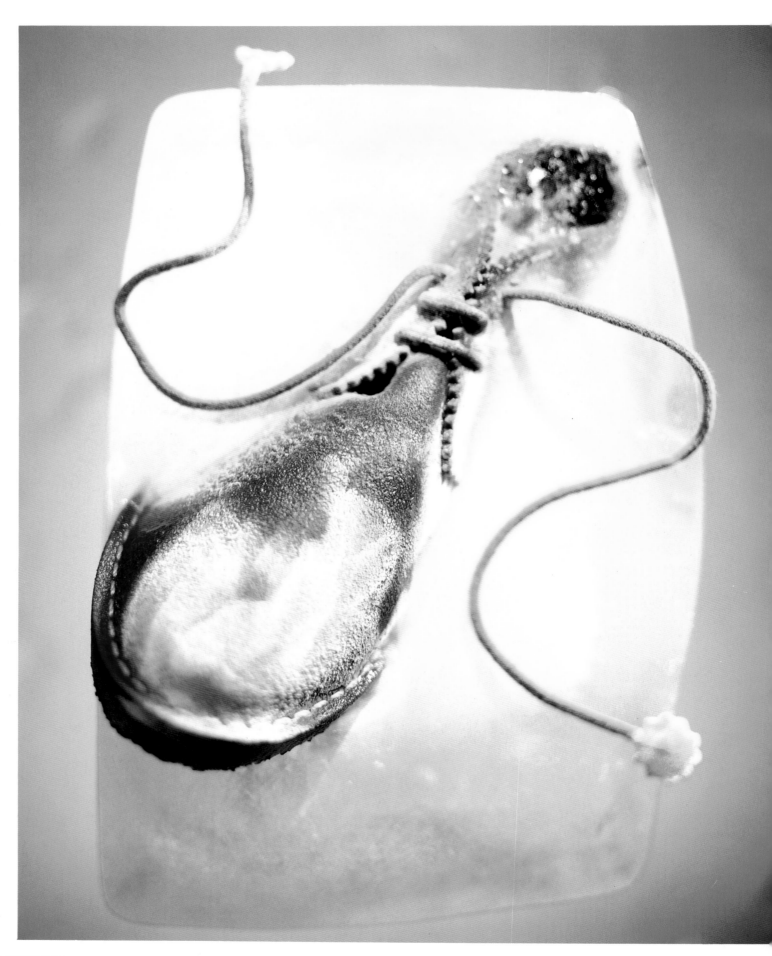

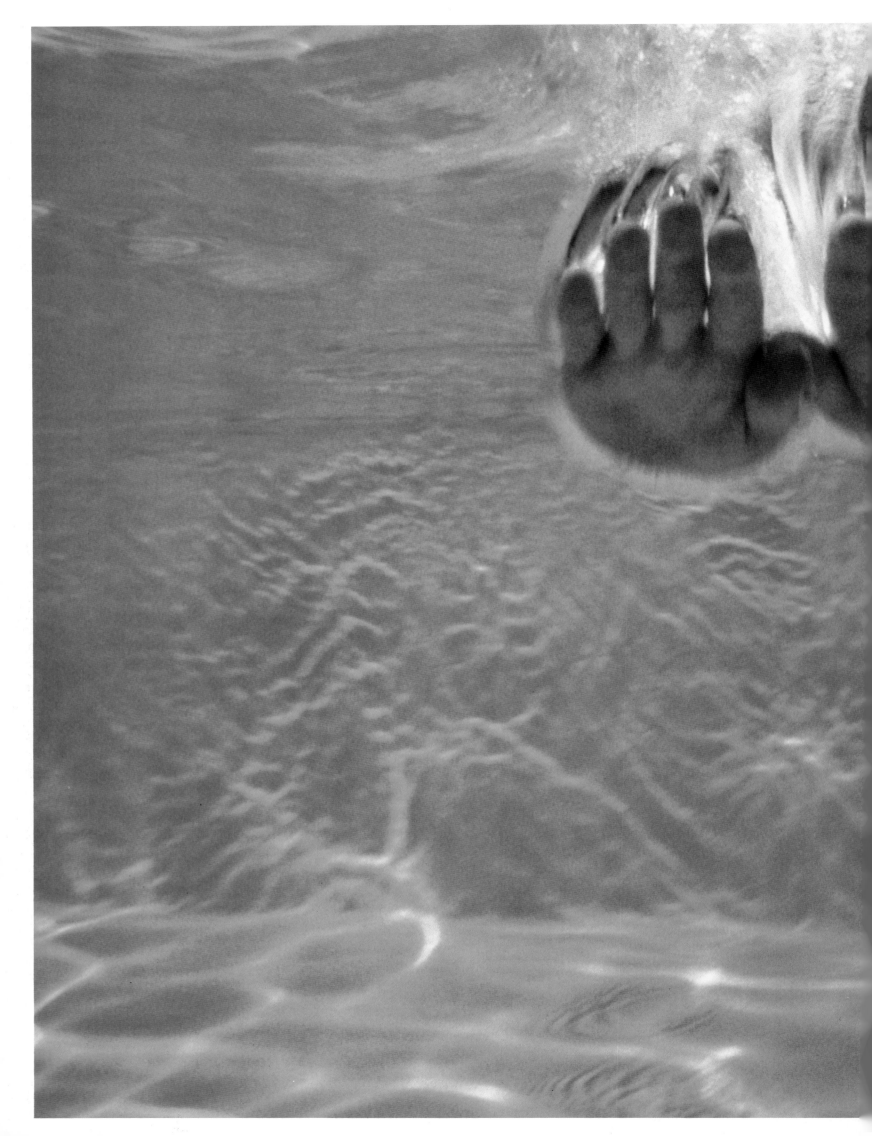

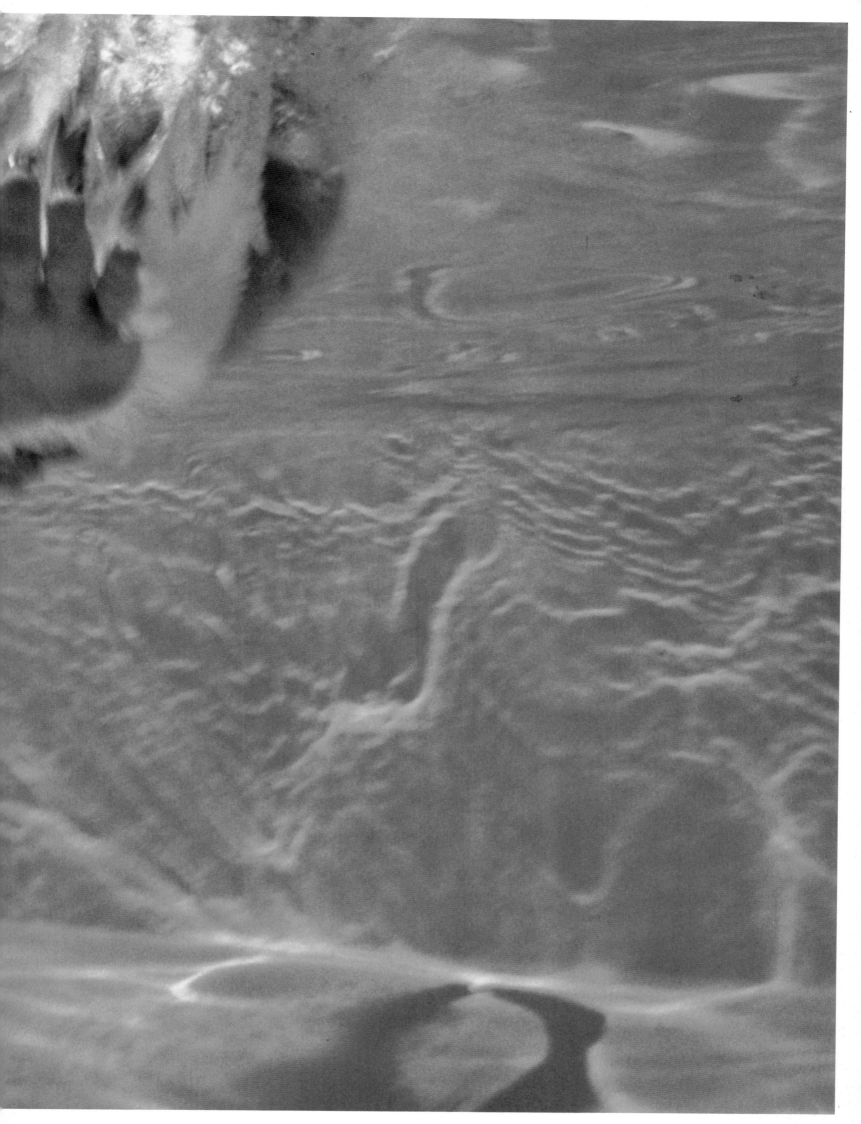

191

192

192 CRAIG CUTLER *PEOPLE IN MOTION.* **193-200 MARY ELLEN MARK** ART DIRECTOR: RAUL MARTINEZ · PHOTO EDITOR: ESIN ILI GÖKNAR · PUBLICATION: VOUGE · PUBLISHER: CONDÉ NAST PUBLICATIONS, INC. · WRITER: DAVID HANDELMAN · (FOLLOWING SERIES) FOR THE FEATURE, *AFTER THE DELUGE*, DECEMBER 1993.

201 JAMES NACHTWEY ASSOCIATE ART DIRECTOR: PAUL LUSSIER • PHOTO EDITOR: MICHELE STEPHENSON • PUBLICATION: TIME • PUBLISHER: TIME INC. • FOR THE ARTICLE, *SUDAN: SLAUGHTER IN SLOW MOTION,* AUGUST 23, 1993. **202 TOM WOLFF** ART DIRECTOR: KELLY DOE • PHOTO EDITOR: KAREN TANAKA • EDITOR: BOB THOMPSON • PUBLICATION: THE WASHINGTON POST MAGAZINE • PUBLISHER: THE WASHINGTON POST COMPANY • WRITER: DAVID FINKEL • COVER PHOTOGRAPH FOR THE FEATURE, *RIVER TRIP-A POTOMAC ODYSSEY,* AUGUST 22, 1993.

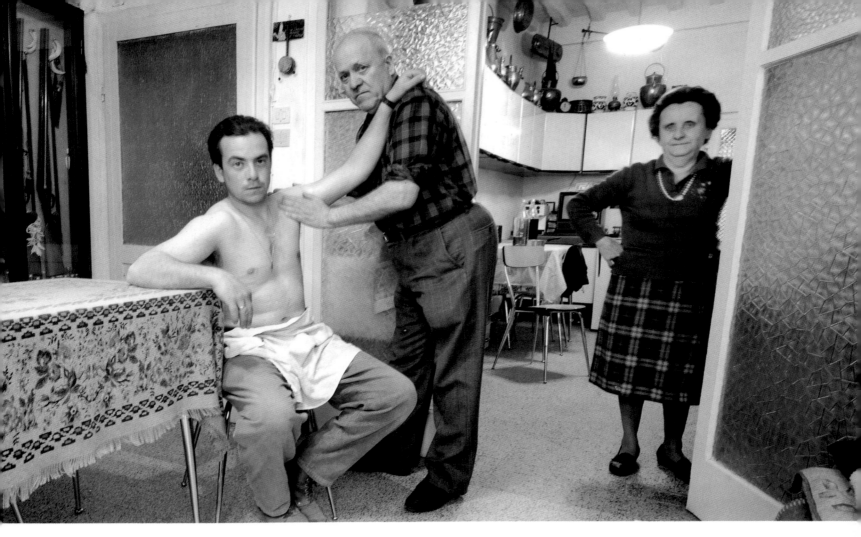

203 BRIAN SMALE ART DIRECTOR: FRED WOODWARD · DESIGNER: GAIL ANDERSON · PHOTO EDITOR: LAURIE KRATOCHVIL · EDITOR: ERIC ETHERIDGE · PUBLICATION: ROLLING STONE · PUBLISHER: WENNER MEDIA, INC. · WRITER: PAUL SOLOTAROFF · FOR THE ARTICLE, *SURVIVING THE CRUSADES*, OCTOBER 14, 1993 **204 DENNIS MARSICO** ART DIRECTOR: LOU DILORENZO · DIRECTOR OF PHOTOGRAPHY: BILL BLACK · PHOTO EDITORS: STEPHANIE SYROP AND KIRSTEN ROHRS · EDITOR: MARGARET STAATS SIMMONS · PUBLICATION: TRAVEL HOLIDAY · PUBLISHER: READER'S DIGEST PUBLICATIONS, INC. · WRITER: SAUL BELLOW · HERBAL HEALER BRUNO PARRI FOR THE FEATURE, *WINTER IN TUSCANY*, NOVEMBER 1992. **205 MARIA ROBLEDO** ART DIRECTOR: GAEL TOWEY · DESIGNER: ANNE JOHNSON · PHOTO EDITOR: GAEL TOWEY · EDITOR: SUSAN WYLAND · PUBLICATION: MARTHA STEWART LIVING · PUBLISHER: TIME INC. · WRITER: CORBY KUMMER · *HOW TO COOK FISH*, APRIL-MAY 1993 (FOLLOWING SPREAD).

206-208 RODNEY SMITH ART DIRECTOR: LESLIE SMOLAN · DESIGNER: JENNIFER DOMER · AUTHORS: RODNEY SMITH AND LESLIE SMOLAN · PUBLISHER: NAN A. TALESE/DOUBLEDAY
· BOOK TITLE: THE HAT BOOK, OCTOBER 1993.

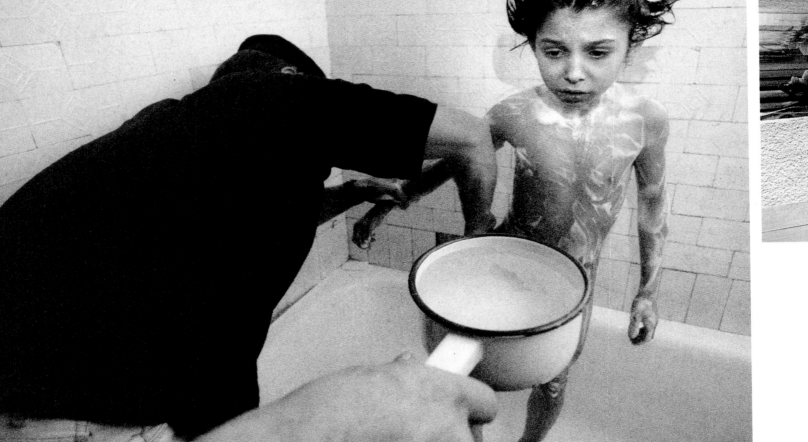

209-211 **JOHN KAPLAN** DESIGNER: CHARLES PATES · PHOTO EDITOR: DAVID FRIEND · PUBLICATION: LIFE · PUBLISHER: TIME INC. · WRITER: JOHN KAPLAN · SERIES OF SERGEI FOR THE ARTICLE, *AN UNTAMED CHILD*, MAY 1993.

212-214 PETER ECKERT UNION STATION, PORTLAND, OR. **215 NIGEL PARRY** ART DIRECTOR: CHARLES CHURCHWARD • PHOTO EDITOR: SUSAN WHITE • EDITOR: ROBERT WALSH • PUBLICATION: VANITY FAIR • PUBLISHER: CONDÉ NAST PUBLICATIONS, INC. • WRITER: ZOE HELLER • WILL SELF FOR THE ARTICLE, *SELF EXAMINATION*, JUNE 1993(FOLLOWING SPREAD).

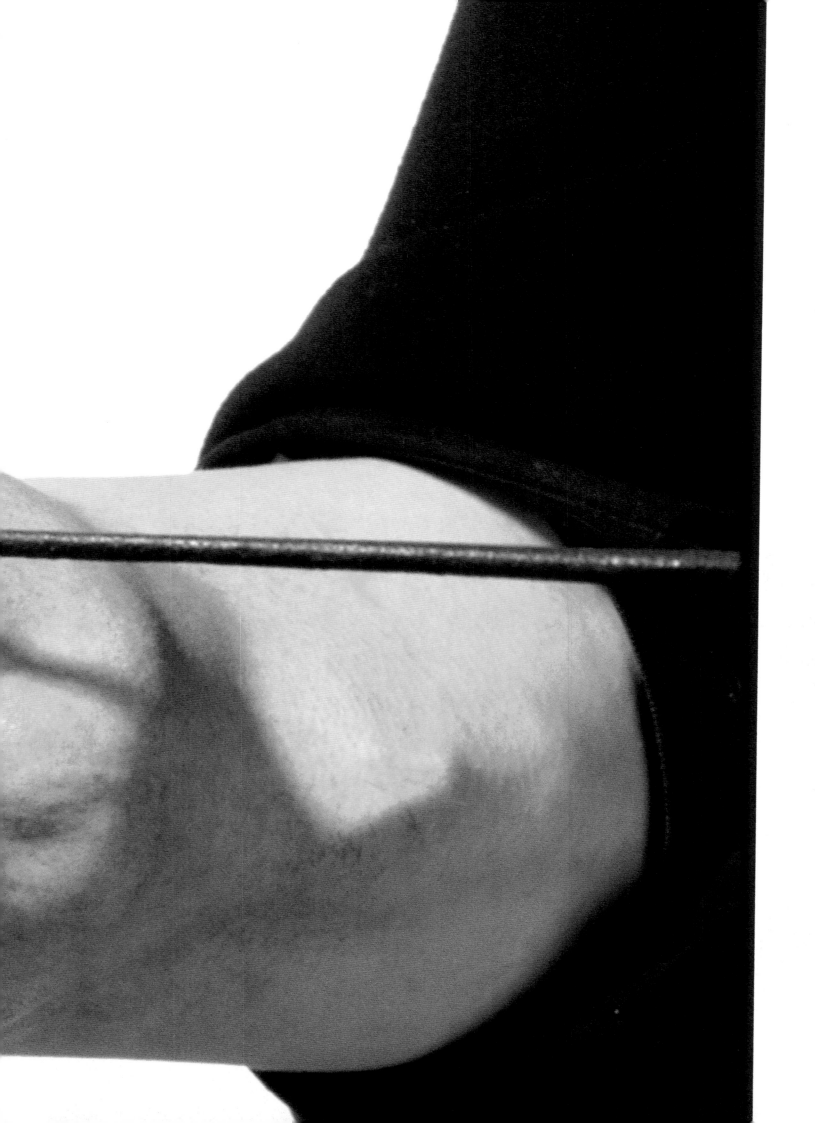

(PRECEDING SPREAD) **216 RAYMOND MEIER** CREATIVE DIRECTOR: FABIEN BARON • ART DIRECTOR: JOEL BERG • PUBLICATION: HARPER'S BAZAAR • PUBLISHER: HEARST PUBLICATIONS • WRITER: AIMEE LEE BALL • FOR THE ARTICLE, *MAN HANDLING*, JUNE 1993. **217 FREDERIK LIEBERATH** CREATIVE DIRECTOR: FABIEN BARON • ART DIRECTOR: JOEL BERG • PUBLICATION: HARPER'S BAZAAR • PUBLISHER: HEARST PUBLICATIONS • WRITER: ELLEN HOPKINS • FOR THE ARTICLE, *CONTRACEPTIVE CHOICE*, FEBRUARY 1993. **218 RAYMOND MEIER** CREATIVE DIRECTOR: FABIEN BARON • ART DIRECTOR: JOEL BERG • PUBLICATION: HARPER'S BAZAAR • PUBLISHER: HEARST PUBLICATIONS • *THE RIGHT SHOE*, APRIL 1993. **219 SUSIE CUSHNER** STYLIST: JACQUELINE LEMIEUX • EDITOR: ELLIOT KRIEGER • PUBLICATION: THE RHODE ISLANDER • PUBLISHER: PROVIDENCE SUNDAY JOURNAL • FOR THE FEATURE, *SUMMER LIVING-INSIDE OUT*, AUGUST 1, 1993.

220 FRANK W. OCKENFELS 3 ART DIRECTOR: MARK ULRIKSEN • PUBLICATION: SAN FRANCISCO FOCUS • PUBLISHER: KQED, INC. • WRITER: FRANK VIVIANO • VIETNAMESE GANG MEMBER FOR THE ARTICLE, *DUST IN THE WIND*, MAY 1993. **221 DAN WINTERS** PHOTO EDITOR: GREG POND • PUBLICATION: DETAILS • PUBLISHER: CONDÉ NAST PUBLICATIONS, INC. • WRITER: DAVID STREITFIELD • AUTHOR WILLIAM GIBSON, OCTOBER 1993 (FOLLOWING SPREAD) **222 JACEK M. KUCY** A VIEW OF THE "LIPSTICK" BUILDING THROUGH THE CITICORP BUILDING. **223 DAN WINTERS** PHOTO EDITOR: GREG POND • PUBLICATION: DETAILS • PUBLISHER: CONDÉ NAST PUBLICATIONS, INC. • WRITER: ROB BUCHANAN • SURFER KELLY SLATER FOR THE ARTICLE, *A BIGGER SPLASH*, MAY 1993.

225

(PRECEDING SPREAD) **224 ALBERT WATSON** PUBLICATION: ROLLING STONE TWENTY FIFTH ANNIVERSARY, PORTRAITS, *DAVID BOWIE* **225 GREGORY HEISLER** CREATIVE DIRECTOR: ROBERT PRIEST • PHOTO EDITOR: KAREN FRANK • EDITOR: LISA HENRICKSSON • PUBLICATION: GQ MAGAZINE • PUBLISHER: CONDÉ NAST PUBLICATIONS, INC. • WRITER: JENNET CONANT • FOR THE ARTICLE, *TOM ARNOLD GETS EVEN*, NOVEMBER 1992. **226 CINDY SHERMAN** CREATIVE DIRECTOR: FABIEN BARON • ART DIRECTOR: JOEL BERG • PUBLICATION: HARPERS BAZAAR • PUBLISHER: HEARST PUBLICATIONS • WRITER: JIM LEWIS • SERIES FOR THE FEATURE, *THE NEW CINDY SHERMAN COLLECTION*, MAY 1993.

228

227 CINDY SHERMAN 228 ANDREW BRUSSO PUBLICATION: ENTERTAINMENT WEEKLY, *WHO'S AFRAID OF HOWARD STERN.*

229, 230 EILEEN HOHMUTH-LEMONICK DESIGNER: KATE TOMPSON • PHOTO EDITOR: TOM MCGOVERN • EDITOR: JONATHAN Z. LARSEN • PUBLICATION: THE VILLAGE VOICE • PUBLISHER: VV PUBLISHING CORPORATION • TEXT BY: VINCE ALETTI • FROM A SERIES ON BLIND INSTITUTIONS ENTITLED *DARKNESS ILLUMINATED*, SEPTEMBER 14, 1993.

231

231 ANTOINE GYORI SARAJEVO: A GRAVEYARD WHERE THE WINTER OLYMPICS WERE ONCE HELD. PHOTOGRAPH COURTESY SYGMA. **232 EILEEN HOHMUTH-LEMONICK** PUBLICATION: THE VILLAGE VOICE, *DARKNESS ILLUMINATED.* **233 ANTONIN KRATOCHVIL** ART DIRECTOR: LOU DILORENZO • DESIGNER: AMY JAFFE • DIRECTOR OF PHOTOGRAPHY: BILL BLACK • PHOTO EDITORS: STEPHANIE SYROP AND KIRSTEN ROHRS • EDITOR: MARGARET STAATS SIMMONS • PUBLICATION: TRAVEL HOLIDAY • PUBLISHER: READER'S DIGEST PUBLICATIONS, INC. • WRITER: ANTONIN KRATOCHVIL • FOR THE FEATURE, *AMERICAN MOMENTS,* DECEMBER 1993 (FOLLOWING SPREAD).

236

234-236 BRUCE BENNETT PUBLICATION: THE NEWS-TIMES SUNDAY MAGAZINE • PUBLISHER: THE NEWS-TIMES, DANBURY, CT • WRITER: FRANK MERKLING • *BENNETT AIMS EYE; OPTIMISM AT ISRAEL*, NOVEMBER 14, 1993. **237-239 JOYCE RAVID** ART DIRECTOR: MATTHEW DRACE • DESIGNER: GIOVANNI RUSSO • PUBLICATION: MEN'S JOURNAL • PUBLISHER: WENNER MEDIA, INC. • WRITER: LAURENCE GONZALES • ROBBIE ROBERTSON IN NEW ORLEANS FOR THE ARTICLE, *SECRETS OF STORYVILLE*, MAY-JUNE 1993 (FOLLOWING SPREAD).

242

240 **CRAIG CUTLER** ART DIRECTOR: BARB PAULINI · AGENCY: HOFFMAN YORK & COMPTON · CLIENT: "VISIONS" WINDOWS · COPYWRITER: DAVID HANNEKEN · COPYLINE: SOME OF THE MORE COMMON NATURAL MATERIALS FOUND IN TODAY'S HOMES. 241 **DAN WINTERS** PUBLICATION: DETAILS, *A BIGGER SPLASH* 242 **DAVID ROSE** ART DIRECTOR: CHARLES CHURCHWARD · PHOTO EDITOR: SUSAN WHITE · EDITORS: MATTHEW TYRNAUER AND AIMEE BELL · PUBLICATION: VANITY FAIR · PUBLISHER: CONDÉ NAST PUBLICATIONS, INC. · WRITER: BILL FLANAGAN · LYLE LOVETT FOR THE ARTICLE, *WE LOVETT!*, SEPTEMBER 1993. 243 **KATHRIN MILLER** ART DIRECTOR: NANCY DUCKWORTH · PHOTO EDITOR: LISA THACKABERRY · EDITOR: BRET ISRAEL · PUBLICATION: LOS ANGELES TIMES MAGAZINE · PUBLISHER: TIMES MIRROR · WRITER: MARGARET L. KNOX · FOR THE ARTICLE, *THE NEW INDIAN WAR*, NOVEMBER 7, 1993.

244 RICHARD ROBINSON ART DIRECTOR: JOHN LYLE SANFORD · EDITOR: REBECCA FARWELL · PUBLICATION: DESTINATION DISCOVERY · PUBLISHER: DISCOVERY COMMUNICATIONS, INC. · WRITER: GARY PARKER · *A JOURNAL FROM THE PLAGUE YEARS, LIFE IN AN AIDS CLINIC,* NOVEMBER 1993. **245,246 DAN WINTERS** ART DIRECTOR: LAURA HARRIGAN · PHOTO EDITOR: KAREN FRANK · PUBLICATION: GQ MAGAZINE · PUBLISHER: CONDÉ NAST PUBLICATIONS, INC. · WRITER: THOMAS MALLON · SERIES FOR THE ARTICLE, *THE NEXT VOICE YOU HEAR,* SEPTEMBER 1993. **247 DAN WINTERS** PHOTOGRAPHY DIRECTOR: MARY DUNN · ASSISTANT PHOTO EDITOR: GEORGE PITTS · PUBLICATION: ENTERTAINMENT WEEKLY · PUBLISHER: TIME INC. · WILLIAM SHATNER FOR THE FEATURE, *I'M TYPING AS FAST AS I CAN,* JANUARY 15, 1993.

248 CRAIG CUTLER 249 MAX AGUILERA-HELLWEG CREATIVE DIRECTOR: ROBERT PRIEST • PHOTO EDITOR: KAREN FRANK • EDITOR: PAUL SCANLON • PUBLICATION: GQ MAGAZINE • PUBLISHER: CONDÉ NAST PUBLICATIONS, INC. • WRITER: JOHN LOMBARDI • DON KING AND JULIO CAESAR CHAVES FOR THE ARTICLE, *KING'S GAMBIT*, MARCH 1993.

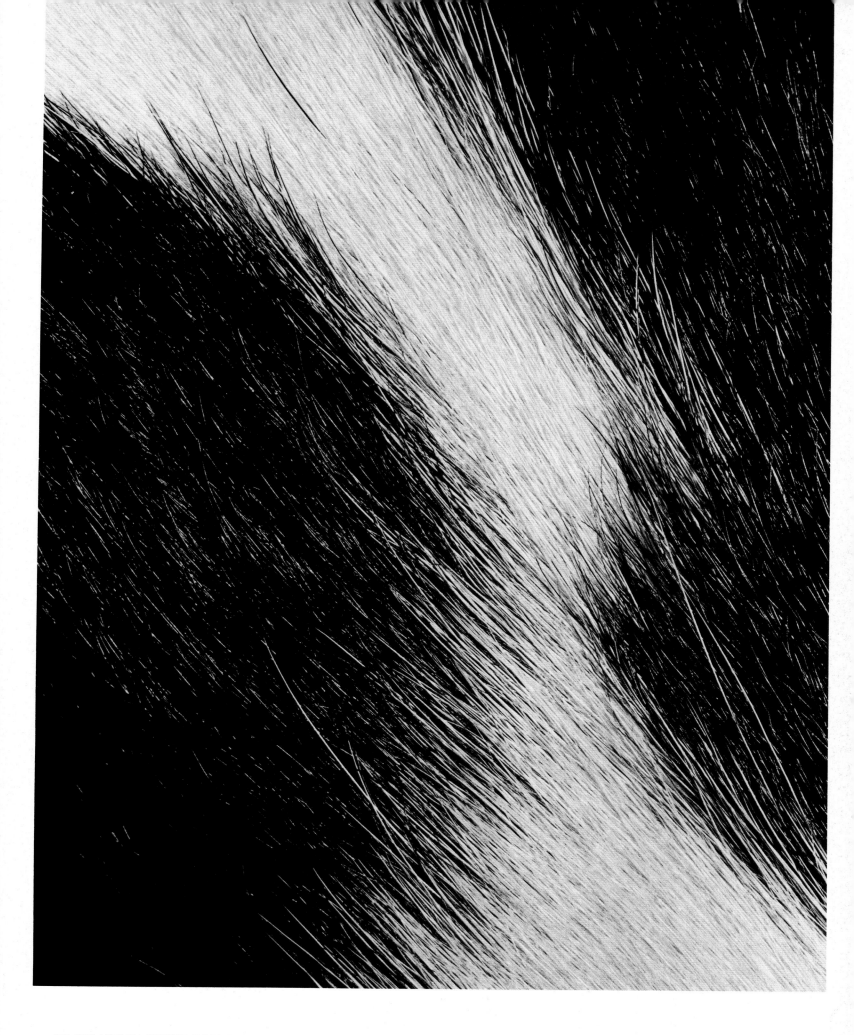

254-256 **BRIAN SMALE** ART DIRECTOR: D.J. STOUT • PHOTO EDITOR: NANCY MCMILLEN • PUBLICATION: TEXAS MONTHLY • PUBLISHER: MEDIATEX COMMUNICATIONS • WRITER: GARY CARTWRIGHT • SERIES OF A MEXICAN BASEBALL TEAM, FOR THE ARTICLE, *CHASING THE RED EAGLE*, AUGUST 1993.

257 VIC HUBER ART DIRECTOR: VIC HUBER • DESIGN FIRM: VIC HUBER PHOTOGRAPHY, INC. • FANGIO 1990 COUPE; PART OF A SELF-PROMOTIONAL CALENDAR. **258 ANNIE LEIBOVITZ** ART DIRECTOR: CHARLES CHURCHWARD • PHOTO EDITOR: SUSAN WHITE • PUBLICATION: VANITY FAIR • PUBLISHER: CONDÉ NAST PUBLICATIONS, INC. • WRITER: RICHARD B. STOLLEY • ALFRED EISENSTADT FOR THE ARTICLE, *ALFRED THE GREAT*, DECEMBER 1993.

259-264 BRIAN SMALE ART DIRECTOR: FRED WOODWARD · PHOTO EDITOR: BOB WALLACE · PUBLICATION: ROLLING STONE · PUBLISHER: WENNER MEDIA, INC. · WRITER: GUY MARTIN · COMMISSIONED, YET NOT PUBLISHED SERIES OF THE UNIFIED GERMAN ARMY.

267 **TIMOTHY HURSLEY** THE JENNINGS OSBORNE FAMILY CHRISTMAS LIGHTS, LITTLE ROCK, AR, 1993.

268 PATRICK ROBERT PHOTO EDITOR: DAVID FRIEND • PUBLICATION: LIFE • PUBLISHER: TIME INC. • FOR THE ARTICLE, *DEADLY DEMONSTRATION*, FEBRUARY 1993.
269 JEFF MERMELSTEIN ART DIRECTOR: JANET FROELICH • PHOTO EDITOR: KATHY RYAN • PUBLICATION: THE NEW YORK TIMES MAGAZINE • PUBLISHER: THE NEW YORK TIMES COMPANY • WRITER: PAUL TOUGH • TEENAGERS "MOSH" AT ROSELAND FOR THE ARTICLE, *INTO THE PIT*, NOVEMBER 7, 1993.

274 DENNIS MARSICO ART DIRECTOR: LOU DILORENZO • DIRECTOR OF PHOTOGRAPHY: BILL BLACK • PHOTO EDITORS: STEPHANIE SYROP AND KIRSTEN ROHRS • EDITOR: MARGARET STAATS SIMMONS • PUBLICATION: TRAVEL HOLIDAY • PUBLISHER: READER'S DIGEST PUBLICATIONS, INC. • WRITER: SAUL BELLOW • FOR THE FEATURE, *WINTER IN TUSCANY*, NOVEMBER 1992.
275 DENNIS MARSICO ART DIRECTOR: LOU DILORENZO • DIRECTOR OF PHOTOGRAPHY: BILL BLACK • PHOTO EDITORS: STEPHANIE SYOP AND KIRSTEN ROHRS • EDITOR: MARGARET STAATS SIMMONS • PUBLICATION: TRAVEL HOLIDAY • PUBLISHER: READER'S DIGEST PUBLICATIONS, INC. • WRITER: BOB SHNAYERSON • FOR THE FEATURE, *THIS WAY TO PARADISE*, MARCH 1993.

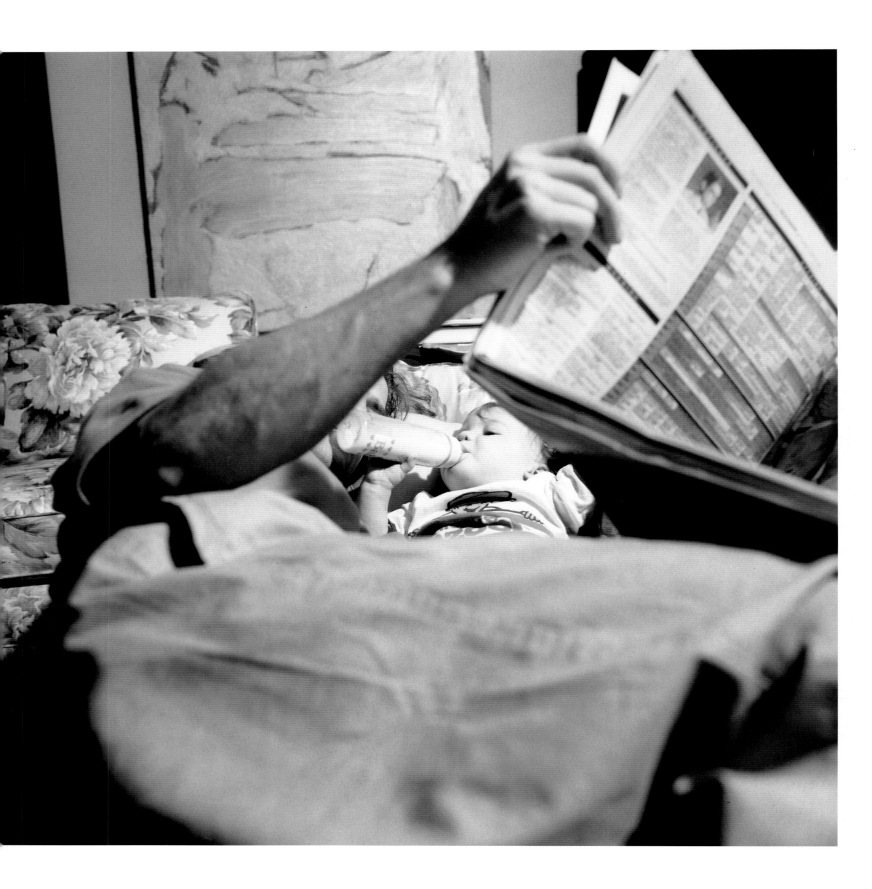

276-277 JEFFREY LOWE ASSOCIATE ART DIRECTOR: PAUL LUSSIER • PHOTO EDITOR: MICHELE STEPHENSON • EDITOR: HOWARD CHUA • PUBLICATION: TIME • PUBLISHER: TIME INC. • WRITER: NANCY R. GIBBS • FOR THE FEATURE, *BRINGING UP FATHER*, JUNE 28, 1993.

278 JEREMY GREEN PART OF A SELF-ASSIGNMENT, *PANAMERICA.* **279 MATUSCHKA** ART DIRECTOR: JANET FROELICH · PHOTO EDITOR: KATHY RYAN · EDITOR: JACK ROSENTHAL · PUBLICATION: THE NEW YORK TIMES MAGAZINE · PUBLISHER: THE NEW YORK TIMES COMPANY · WRITER: SUSAN FERRARO · *BEAUTY OUT OF DAMAGE,* FOR THE ARTICLE, *YOU CAN'T LOOK AWAY ANYMORE,* AUGUST 5, 1993.

284 DAN WINTERS ART DIRECTOR: MICHAEL GROSSMAN • PHOTOGRAPHY DIRECTOR: MARY DUNN • ASSISTANT PHOTO EDITOR: MARK JACOBSON •
PUBLICATION: ENTERTAINMENT WEEKLY • PUBLISHER: TIME INC. • DR. DRE FOR THE FEATURE, *ENTERTAINERS OF THE YEAR*, DECEMBER 31, 1993.
285 KURT MARKUS ROLLING STONE TWENTY FIFTH ANNIVERSARY, PORTRAITS, *B.B. KING*

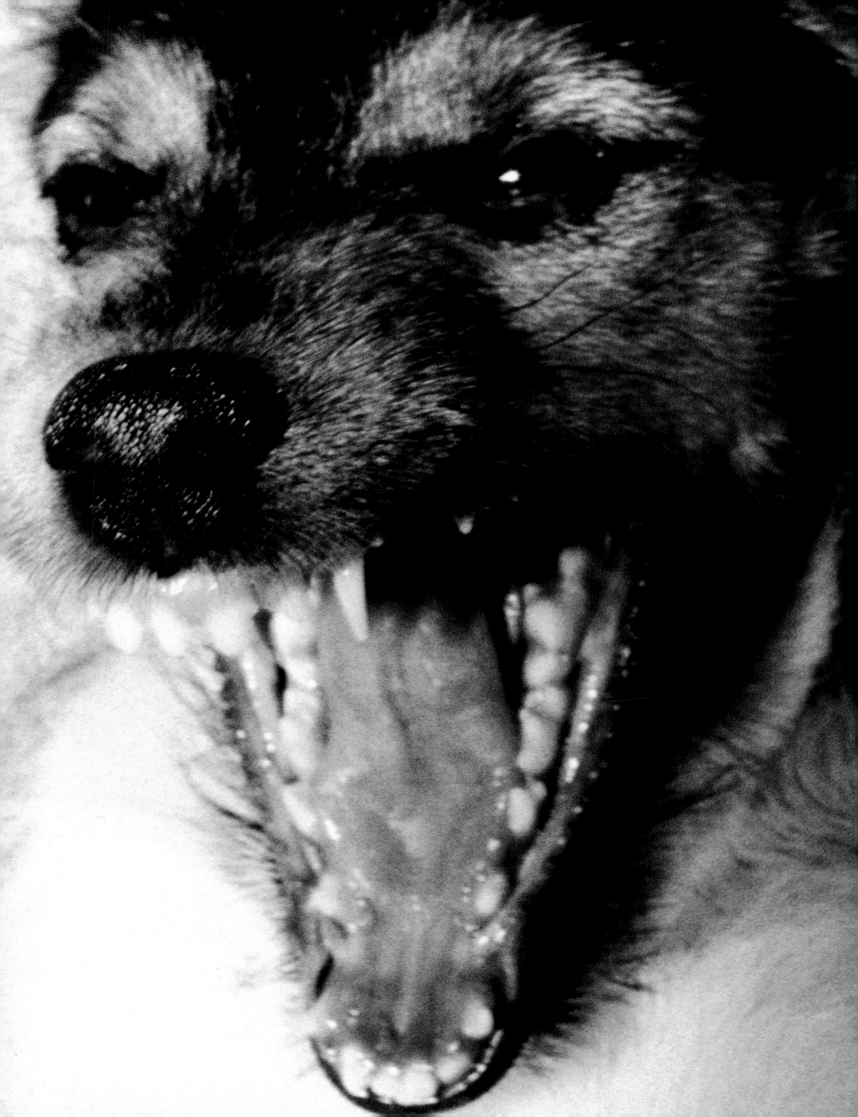

289

287 **GABRIELLA IMPERATORI** FROM THE SERIES, *BEAUTY AND THE BEAST.* 288,289 **MARK SELIGER** ART DIRECTOR: FRED WOODWARD • DESIGNERS: FRED WOODWARD AND GAIL ANDERSON • PHOTO EDITOR: LAURIE KRATOCHVIL • EDITOR: SID HOLT • PUBLICATION: ROLLING STONE • PUBLISHER: WENNER MEDIA, INC. • WRITER: DAVID FRICKE • SERIES OF METALLICA'S JAMES HETFIELD, APRIL 15, 1993. 290-292 **DAVID LACHAPELLE** PUBLICATION: DETAILS, *FAMILY MATTERS.*

293

293, 294 **EILEEN HOHMUTH-LEMONICK** PUBLICATION: THE VILLAGE VOICE, *DARKNESS ILLUMINATED.* **295 CHRISTINA GARCIA RODÉRO** PUBLICATION: THE LOS ANGELES TIMES MAGAZINE, *THE RITES OF SPRING* (FOLLOWING SPREAD).

296, 297 ANTON CORBIJN PHOTO EDITOR: GREG POND · PUBLICATION: DETAILS · PUBLISHER: CONDÉ NAST PUBLICATIONS, INC. · WRITER: CHRIS HEATH · MICHAEL STIPE AND R.E.M FOR THE ARTICLE, *ENIGMATIC FOR THE PEOPLE*, FEBRUARY 1993. **298-303 FRANK W. OCKENFELS 3** PRODUCER: DEBORAH ROSEN · PRODUCTION COMPANY: ROSEN & COMPANY · TITLE OF FEATURE: THE QUIET ROOM · FOR THE SHOWTIME SERIES, FALLEN ANGELS.

304-305 **RICHARD AVEDON** DESIGNER: MARY SHANAHAN · EDITOR: TINA BROWN · PUBLICATION: THE NEW YORKER · *THE FACES OF ANGELS.* THE *ANGELS IN AMERICA* COMPANY: DIRECTOR GEORGE C. WOLFE. LEFT TO RIGHT: KATHLEEN CHALFANT (HANNAH PITT), JEFFREY WRIGHT (BELIZE), DAVID MARSHALL GRANT (JOE PITT), MARCIA GAY HARDEN (HARPER PITT), AND STEPHEN SPINELLA (PRIOR WALTER). **306-307** **RICHARD AVEDON** DESIGNER: MARY SHANAHAN · EDITOR: TINA BROWN · PUBLICATION: THE NEW YORKER · LEFT TO RIGHT: STEPHEN SPINELLA (PRIOR WALTER), JOE MANTELLO (LOUIS IRONSON), ELLEN MCLAUGHLIN (THE ANGEL), AND RON LEIBMAN (ROY COHN). PLAYWRIGHT, TONY KUSHNER (FOLLOWING SPREAD).

310

309, 310 **ALBERT WATSON** ROLLING STONE TWENTY FIFTH ANNIVERSARY, PORTRAITS, *AL GREEN, NEIL YOUNG* 311 **MATTHEW ROLSTON** ROLLING STONE TWENTY FIFTH ANNIVERSARY, PORTRAITS, *YOKO ONO*

312 **ALBERT WATSON** PUBLICATION: ROLLING STONE TWENTY FIFTH ANNIVERSARY, PORTRAITS, *ERIC CLAPTON* **313-358** **RICHARD AVEDON** DESIGNER: MARY SHANAHAN • EDITOR: TINA BROWN • PUBLICATION: THE NEW YORKER • *EXILES: THE KENNEDY COURT AT THE END OF THE AMERICAN CENTURY* • "IN JANUARY OF 1961, JUST BEFORE JOHN KENNEDY'S INAUGURATION, I DID A SERIES OF PORTRAITS OF HIM AND HIS FAMILY AT THEIR HOUSE IN PALM BEACH. THE KENNEDYS AND MANY OF THE PEOPLE THEY ATTRACTED WERE FULL OF PROMISE AND PRIDE, AND THEY HAD A RESPECT FOR INTELLECT THAT I HAVEN'T SEEN AGAIN IN AMERICAN POLITICS. FROM JULY 8TH TO SEPTEMBER 14TH OF 1993, I TRAVELED ACROSS THE COUNTRY TO PHOTOGRAPH SURVIVING MEN AND WOMEN OF THAT PERIOD-PEOPLE MOSTLY OF MY GENERATION, WHO FOR A WHILE HAD FAITH IN POWER." **313** THE PRESIDENT-ELECT AND MRS. KENNEDY, *PALM BEACH, 1961.* **314** CAROLINE KENNEDY AND JOHN KENNEDY, JR., *PALM BEACH, 1961.* **315** JOHN GLENN IN 1961. *FIRST AMERICAN TO ORBIT THE EARTH.* **316** JOHN GLENN IN 1993. *DEMOCRATIC SENATOR FROM OHIO.* **317** DAVE POWERS. SPECIAL ASSISTANT TO THE PRESIDENT. *MUSEUM CURATOR OF THE JOHN F. KENNEDY LIBRARY, IN DORCHESTER, MASSACHUSETTS. RETIRED, 1994.* **318** EUNICE KENNEDY SHRIVER. *SISTER OF THE PRESIDENT FOUNDER AND HONORARY CHAIRMAN OF SPECIAL OLYMPICS INTERNATIONAL* **319** CLARK CLIFFORD. INFORMAL ADVISER AND LAWYER TO THE PRESIDENT; SECRETARY OF DEFENSE, 1968-69. RETIRED. **320** DEAN RUSK. SECRETARY OF STATE. NOW PROFESSOR OF INTERNATIONAL LAW EMERITUS AT THE UNIVERSITY OF GEORGIA. **321** JULIAN BOND IN 1993. COMMUNICATIONS DIRECTOR, STUDENT NON-VIOLENT COORDINATING COMMITTEE. GEORGIA STATE LEGISLATOR, 1965-87. NOW LECTURER IN HISTORY AT THE UNIVERSITY OF VIRGINIA AND ADJUNCT PROFESSOR AT AMERICAN UNIVERSITY. **322** JULIAN BOND IN 1963. **323** EVELYN LINCOLN. PERSONAL SECRETARY TO THE PRESIDENT. RETIRED. **324** FRANK SINATRA. FUND-RAISER, CAMPAIGNER, FRIEND. **325** WILLIAM MANCHESTER. AUTHOR OF "PORTRAIT OF A PRESIDENT" (1962) AND "DEATH OF A PRESIDENT" (1967). NOW ADJUNCT PROFESSOR OF HISTORY EMERITUS AND WRITER-IN-RESIDENCE AT WESLEYAN UNIVERSITY. **326** RICHARD GOODWIN. CAMPAIGN SPEECHWRITER; SPECIAL ASSISTANT TO THE PRESIDENT FOR LATIN-AMERICAN AFFAIRS. AUTHOR, MOST RECENTLY, OF "REMEMBERING AMERICA: A VOICE FROM THE SIXTIES." **327** JOHN DOAR, FIRST ASSISTANT, CIVIL RIGHTS DIVISION, DEPARTMENT OF JUSTICE. NOW A PARTNER IN A NEW YORK LAW FIRM. JAMES MEREDITH. FIRST BLACK STUDENT TO ATTEND THE UNIVERSITY OF MISSISSIPPI. NOW A WRITER IN JACKSON, MISSISSIPPI. NICHOLAS KATZENBACH. DEPUTY ATTORNEY GENERAL. NOW OF COUNSEL IN A NEW JERSEY LAW FIRM. **328** GEORGE WALLACE, WITH HIS VALET, JIMMY DALLAS. GOVERNOR OF ALABAMA. NOW CHAIRMAN OF THE DEPARTMENT OF PUBLIC ADMINISTRATION AT TROY STATE UNIVERSITY. **329** JOSEPH P. KENNEDY II. NEPHEW OF THE PRESIDENT; OLDEST SON OF ROBERT F. KENNEDY. DEMOCRATIC REPRESENTATIVE FROM THE EIGHT CONGRESSIONAL DISTRICT IN MASSACHUSETTS, THE SEAT HELD BEFORE HIM BY, SUCCESSIVELY, HIS UNCLE AND TIP O'NEILL. **330** ETHEL KENNEDY. WIFE OF ROBERT F. KENNEDY. FOUNDING MEMBER OF THE ROBERT F. KENNEDY MEMORIAL. **331** KERRY KENNEDY CUOMO. DAUGHTER OF ROBERT F. KENNEDY. FOUNDER AND EXECUTIVE DIRECTOR OF THE ROBERT F. KENNEDY MEMORIAL CENTER FOR HUMAN RIGHTS. **332** JOHN LEWIS. CHAIRMAN, STUDENT NON-VIOLENT COORDINATING COMMITTEE. DEMOCRATIC REPRESENTATIVE FROM THE FIFTH CONGRESSIONAL DISTRICT IN GEORGIA. **333** TOM MILANO'S BAR & GRILL, HOUSTON STREET, NEW YORK, AUGUST 29, 1993. **334** ROBERT MCNAMARA. SECRETARY OF DEFENSE. PRESIDENT, THE WORLD BANK, 1968-81. CURRENTLY WRITING HIS AUTOBIOGRAPHY. **335** BURKE MARSHALL. ASSISTANT ATTORNEY GENERAL, CIVIL RIGHTS DIVISION, DEPARTMENT OF JUSTICE. NOW PROFESSOR OF LAW EMERITUS AT YALE LAW SCHOOL. **336** SARGENT SHRIVER. FOUNDING DIRECTOR OF THE PEACE CORPS. DEMOCRATIC VICE-PRESIDENT CANDIDATE, 1972. NOW CHAIRMAN OF THE BOARD, SPECIAL OLYMPICS INTERNATIONAL. **337** BENJAMIN C. BRADLEE. FRIEND OF THE PRESIDENT; WASHINGTON BUREAU CHIEF, "NEWSWEEK." FORMER EXECUTIVE EDITOR OF THE "WASHINGTON POST," AND NOW VICE-PRESIDENT AT LARGE. **338** THOMAS P. (TIP) O'NEILL. THE PRESIDENT'S SUCCESSOR AS REPRESENTATIVE FROM THE EIGHTH CONGRESSIONAL DISTRICT OF MASSACHUSETTS. SPEAKER OF THE HOUSE, 1977-1986. DIED JANUARY 5, 1994. **339** HARRIS WOFFORD. SPECIAL ASSISTANT TO THE PRESIDENT FOR CIVIL RIGHTS. PRESIDENT, BRYN MAWR COLLEGE, 1970-78. ELECTED SENATOR FROM PENNSYLVANIA, 1991. **340** ARTHUR SCHLESINGER, JR. SPEECHWRITER; SPECIAL ASSISTANT TO THE PRESIDENT. AUTHOR AND HUMANITIES PROFESSOR AT THE CITY UNIVERSITY OF NEW YORK. **341, 342.** MALCOLM BROWNE, PETER ARNETT, HORST HAAS, DAVID HALBERSTAM, NEIL SHEEHAN. PULITZER PRIZE WINNERS, ALL FOR THEIR WORK ON THE VIETNAM WAR. **343** PIERRE SALINGER.PRESIDENTIAL PRESS SECRETARY; APPOINTED SENATOR FROM CALIFORNIA, 1964. NOW VICE-CHAIRMAN, BURSON-MARSTELLER. **344** BETTY BEALE. SOCIETY COLUMNIST, THE WASHINGTON "EVENING STAR." AUTHOR OF "POWER AT PLAY: A MEMOIR OF PARTIES, POLITICIANS, AND THE PRESIDENTS IN MY BEDROOM." **345** THEODORE C. SORENSEN. SPEECHWRITER; COUNSEL TO THE PRESIDENT. SINCE 1966, A PARTNER IN THE LAW FIRM PAUL, WEISS, RIFKIND, WHARTON & GARRISON, IN NEW YORK. **346** MCGEORGE BUNDY. SPECIAL ASSISTANT TO THE PRESIDENT FOR NATIONAL SECURITY AFFAIRS. NOW SCHOLAR-IN-RESIDENCE AT THE CARNEGIE CORPORATION OF NEW YORK. **347** TOM HAYDEN IN 1969. CO-FOUNDER, STUDENTS FOR A DEMOCRATIC SOCIETY. **348** TOM HAYDEN IN 1993. CALIFORNIA STATE SENATOR. **349** ABRAHAM RIBICOFF. SECRETARY OF HEALTH, EDUCATION, AND WELFARE. GOVERNOR OF CONNECTICUT, 1956-61. PARTNER IN THE LAW FIRM KAYE, SCHOLER, FIERMAN, HAYS & HANDLER, IN NEW YORK. **350** JOHN KENNETH GALBRAITH. ECONOMIC ADVISER; AMBASSADOR TO INDIA. PAUL M. WARBURG PROFESSOR OF ECONOMICS EMERITUS AT HARVARD. **351** BARRY GOLDWATER. REPUBLICAN SENATOR FROM ARIZONA; FRIEND AND POLITICAL OPPONENT OF THE PRESIDENT. RETIRED. **352** THE REVEREND MARTIN LUTHER KING; THE REVEREND MARTIN LUTHER KING, JR.; MARTIN LUTHER KING III IN 1963. **353** JAMES RESTON. WASHINGTON BUREAU CHIEF, THE NEW YORK "TIMES." SENIOR COLUMNIST AT THE "TIMES." **354** J. WILLIAM FULBRIGHT. DEMOCRATIC SENATOR FROM ARKANSAS; CHAIRMAN, SENATE FOREIGN RELATIONS COMMITTEE. RETIRED. **355** DANIEL PATRICK MOYNIHAN. ASSISTANT SECRETARY OF LABOR. DEMOCRATIC SENATOR FROM NEW YORK; CHAIRMAN, SENATE FINANCE COMMITTEE. **356** TIMES SQUARE, NEW YORK, NOVEMBER 22, 1963. **357** ROSE KENNEDY IN 1976. NOW A HUNDRED AND FOUR, STILL RESIDES IN HYANNIS PORT, MASSACHUSETTS. **358** T-SHIRT IN GRAND CENTRAL TERMINAL, NEW YORK, SEPTEMBER 9, 1993.

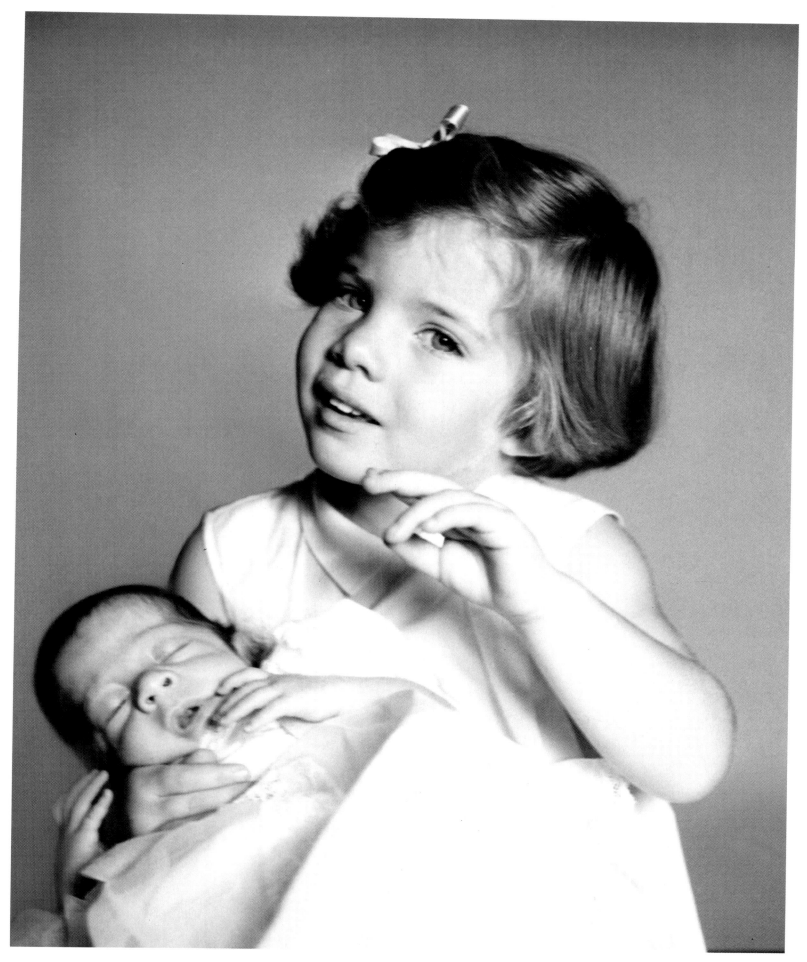

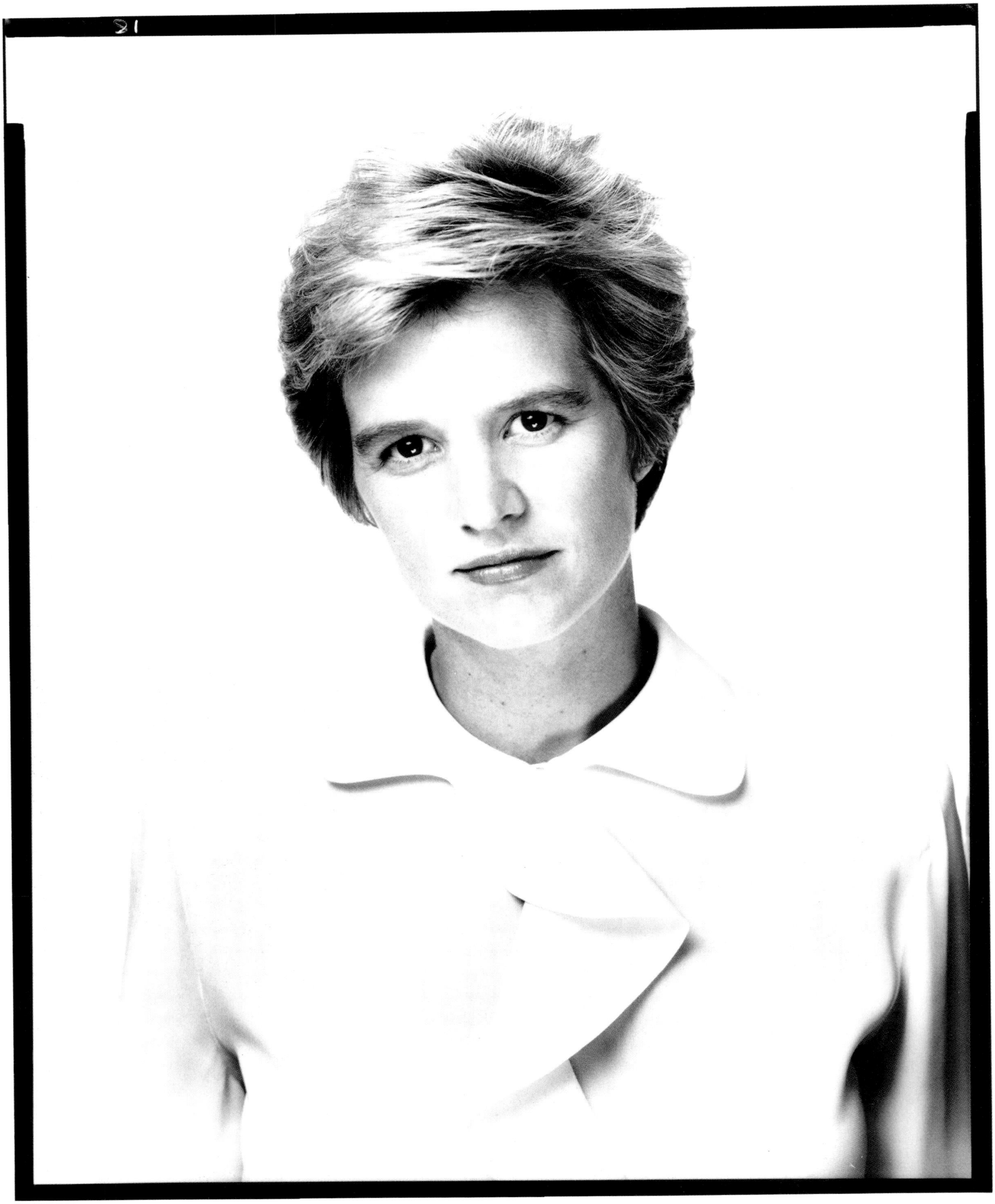
21

335

336

337

338

339

340

341

342

New York World-Telegram
and
The Sun

PRESIDENT
SHOT DEAD
EXTRA

7 SPORTS
WALL ST.
LATEST PRICES

Market Is Jittery
Over Suspension
Declines
Follow
Early Rise
Martinis Battled
Photog, Cop Says

Epstein Due
To Give Up
On Tuesday

ART DIRECTORS, CREATIVE DIRECTORS AND DESIGNERS

PHOTOGRAPHY EDITORS

EDITORS

PUBLICATIONS